Preaching in Place

LLOYD JOHN OGILVIE INSTITUTE
OF PREACHING SERIES

SERIES EDITORS:
Mark Labberton
Clayton J. Schmit

The vision of the Lloyd John Ogilvie Institute of Preaching is to proclaim Jesus Christ and to catalyze a movement of empowered, wise preachers who seek justice, love mercy, and walk humbly with God, leading others to join in God's mission in the world. The books in this series are selected to contribute to the development of such wise and humble preachers. The authors represent both scholars of preaching as well as pastors and preachers whose experiences and insights can contribute to passionate and excellent preaching.

OTHER VOLUMES IN THIS SERIES:

The Eloquence of Grace: Joseph Sittler and the Preaching Life edited by James M. Childs Jr. and Richard Lischer

The Preacher as Liturgical Artist: Metaphor, Idenitity, and the Vicarious Humanity of Christ by Trygve David Johnson

Ordinary Preacher, Extraordinary Gospel: A Daily Guide for Wise, Empowered Preachers by Chris Neufeld-Erdman

Bringing Home the Message: How Community Can Multiply the Power of the Preached Word by Robert K. Perkins

Decolonizing Preaching: The Pulpit as Postcolonial Space by Sarah A. N. Travis

Preaching in Place

Wendell Berry and the Agrarian Sermon

Mark R. Rigg

CASCADE *Books* • Eugene, Oregon

PREACHING IN PLACE
Wendell Berry and the Agrarian Sermon

Lloyd John Ogilvie Institute of Preaching Series

Cascade Books
An Imprint of Wipf and Stock Publishers
199 W. 8th Ave., Suite 3
Eugene, OR 97401

www.wipfandstock.com

PAPERBACK ISBN: 978-1-6667-3263-4
HARDCOVER ISBN: 978-1-6667-2655-8
EBOOK ISBN: 978-1-6667-2656-5

Cataloguing-in-Publication data:

Names: Rigg, Mark R.

Title: Preaching in place : Wendell Berry and the agrarian sermon / Mark R. Rigg.

Description: Eugene, OR: Cascade Books, 2022 | Series: Lloyd John Ogilvie Institute
of Preaching Series | Includes bibliographical references.

Identifiers: ISBN 978-1-6667-3263-4 (paperback) | ISBN 978-1-6667-2655-8 (hard-
cover) | ISBN 978-1-6667-2656-5 (ebook)

Subjects: Berry, Wendell, 1934- | Preaching.

Classification: BV4211.3 R5 2022 (print) | BV4211.3 (ebook)

For Glenn

Table of Contents

Acknowledgments

A LARGE AND GRACIOUS group of people has made this book possible. The membership of Advent Lutheran Church, West Lawn, Pennsylvania, helped finance my writing over the course of several years. They were the first community for whom this book was written. May God bless them. Sue and Mary and Paul supported my labors and each other when I was occupied with the writing. A great cloud of friends listened patiently and encouragingly; among them must be named Steve, Melinda and Fred, Ty and Mary, and Amy. My gratitude to Clay for his encouragement is immense. Finally, the reflections contained herein saw the first light of day in doctoral work at Luther Seminary in St. Paul, Minnesota. I give thanks for the faithfulness of my colleagues in the cohort and for the professors who worked with us.

1

The Importance of Remembering

THE PROBLEM OF DISLOCATION

This book had its genesis long before I was aware of it. More than a decade ago I was studying for a seminary degree when I began to recognize connections between my theological readings and the writings of Wendell Berry, an author whose essays, fiction, and verse had already been a staple of my intellectual life for many years. I found that two parts of my mind that had hitherto seemed distinct and only distantly related had in fact a common border, even some shared terrain.

In particular, I was noticing correlations between Berry's understanding of a farm and my own understanding of church and of congregation. The following words—found in Berry's essay "Faustian Economics"—were the paragraph that brought to conscious awareness the interrelationships I had been sensing:

> Our human and earthly limits, properly understood, are not confinements but rather inducements to formal elaboration and elegance, to fullness of relationship and meaning. Perhaps our most serious cultural loss in recent centuries is the knowledge that some things, though limited, are inexhaustible. For example, an ecosystem, even that of a working forest or farm, so long as it remains ecologically intact, is inexhaustible. A small place, as I know from my own experience, can provide opportunities of work and learning, and a fund of beauty, solace, and pleasure—in

addition to its difficulties—that cannot be exhausted in a lifetime or in generations.[1]

In a moment of quiet epiphany, I realized that Berry's words apply to a congregation much as they apply to a farm. Congregations have been for centuries limited but inexhaustible systems—places of seasons and cycles, of eternal promise contained in earthly frames, of "formal elaboration and elegance" rather than of worldly success or progress. As such, congregations—like farms—offer us an alternative vision to that of the dominant powers and culture.

Such an alternative seems to me especially important as we recognize that mainline congregations are increasingly alien to their own place. While they love their buildings, they are often not meaningfully connected to them. Almost entirely a memory is the time when people lived in the same neighborhood or even the same town as their congregation of choice. There are, of course, exceptions—the urban church that draws from its densely populated locale, the country church where worship options are few. However, it is so common as to go unnoticed that vast numbers of American Christians drive to their congregation, often significant distances, often past many other church buildings. What is more, they are unlikely to be connected to the community around the congregation in ways beyond "good works" such as food pantries or clothing drives. In short, a great many American Christians in the early twenty-first century are dislocated: they are not connected to their congregation—or, by extension, their faith—by traditional bonds of proximity or neighborliness.

Such dislocation exacerbates the misunderstanding many people harbor that a congregation is a voluntary association of like-minded individuals. Rather than seeing themselves called by God to worship and work in a particular time and place, they are increasingly likely to understand themselves as acquaintances who are purchasing and consuming a religious product. Just as we drive to the restaurant or the store or the strip mall, so we drive to church. When we get to any of these places, the paid professionals provide services we want, and then we return to our homes, our "real" places. The problem of dislocation, then, is that it attenuates our basic understanding of what Christian community is.

1. Berry, *World-Ending Fire*, 217–18.

JUSTIFICATION AND RATIONALE

It is worth pausing to reflect why the works of Wendell Berry, a farmer, a sometime Baptist, and a vocal critic of many of the practices of American churches, are—or ought to be—important to people of various Christian communities and to the life of the larger church.

The importance of coming to grips with the works of Wendell Berry might be thought of under the rubric of "remembering." One of Berry's novels bears this name, *Remembering*, and it is clear in the novel and in various essays that Berry has a double meaning in mind when he uses that word. Neither meaning, interestingly, is much related to our basic sense of the word "remember" as simply "to recall" or "to think back on." Rather, by remembering Berry first means becoming connected with those who have come before us—becoming once again conscious of a membership that precedes us and that bequeaths to us, along with a fair share of human sin and folly, practices and practical wisdom that we do well to heed. Engaging with Berry, then, is a beginning—a way of re-membering in our work those who have gone before: the saints in general, the theologians and pastors and church workers who have taught us, and the lines of family that stretch back through the generations. My people, for example, have been in North America for more than 400 years, most of that time as farmers themselves. I am the inheritor of any number of stories that occur on "the family place" outside the small towns of Ohio and Indiana where my people come from. Berry offers a way to remember and be "re-membered" with many who have gone before.

Berry's second sense of remembering has to do with connecting with the people in our own communities—church communities and local municipalities. Berry's prose is full of biblical allusions and is undergirded by biblical motifs and narrative structures; when he speaks of the people of his fictional town, Port William, as "the membership," he is using that term in much the way the New Testament speaks of the saints or of the local congregation. So, in our ministries, it is vital to be regularly reminded that we are members of one another and of Christ's church.

If this book is useful at all, its usefulness will be found within a particular setting and ministry context. Berry's writing reframes most of the issues confronting the fairly traditional mainline congregations that dot our landscape. His emphasis on the local community as the center of its own attention provides a powerful antidote for any congregation that wishes to be something else, whether that "else" is found in the congregation's idealized past or imagined future or whether it is found in a cultural model unsuited to its actual time and place. Berry's mistrust of technology as the answer to relational problems speaks a word of peace to a congregation tempted to believe that a better website or Facebook account will bring new (and better!) members into the community. His emphasis on making economic questions central and on placing a premium on the small and the local— valuing what the larger culture does not—provides a model of faithfulness that congregations need in a time when they are culturally less and less central. Finally—and this will be argued in far greater detail below—these very themes shape an agrarian theology of preaching.

As to the question of how this book might be of value to the larger Christian community, I am cautious about speculating. Such caution comes not from an actual or false modesty but is rather part and parcel of the project itself. As Berry reminds us repeatedly, it is fundamental to western, capitalistic, democratic worldviews to presume to think and speak and act for others. There are both conservative and liberal versions of this presumption; but, in any case, the desire to think globally and act locally almost invariably proceeds from an unreflective Enlightenment confidence that local concerns are best addressed by large-scale national or even global answers. Global economies, global militaries, global finances: it is stunning both how dependent we are on all of these realities and also how little con-sideration is given to the cost in land and lives and communities that these large-scale realities exact. In the face of such unconscious dependence, Berry's counter-mantra—think locally, act locally—is both startling and potentially liberating.

What if, instead of asking how these ideas might be important to the larger church, we asked the question this way: how might different local communities respond in their own ways to an agrarian ecclesiology and homiletic? Then, of course, the first answer would necessarily be, "We do not know." Such confident ignorance helpfully acknowledges that one person in the midst of one Christian community cannot think, speak, or act for other people and Christian communities. Or, to put it more positively, this work proposes to prompt questions and reflection rather than to provide answers; the hope is that such reflection leads others to understanding and action appropriate to their own time and place.

Ignorance, then, properly understood, is a gift. It curtails specula-tion and presumption in a way that is reminiscent of the theology of the cross. Instead of speculating, we find ourselves in the position of needing one another, of saying, "Here is how agrarian ecclesiology works in my community. How does it work in yours?" In this way, the larger church is not an abstraction but is instead what it actually is—an interrelationship of local communities made one body in Jesus Christ.

WENDELL BERRY FOR BEGINNERS

Wendell Berry has written over forty books. They are fairly evenly spread among three fields: fiction, poetry, and essays. The fiction itself is split between seven major novels and dozens of short stories. Both the novels and the short stories are centered almost entirely in the fictional town of Port William, Kentucky, a capacious reimagining of Berry's own hometown of Port Royal, Kentucky. His essays are agrarian in nature, tackling a wide range of topics but always coming back to questions of creation, community, farming, and economics. His poetry is generally an outdoor poetry, and he is especially known for his Sabbath poems, writing that he does in response to his long Sunday walks.

It is of course impossible in a volume of this length to catalogue, let alone describe, the breadth and depth of his writing. He has been writing since he was a young man, and he is now in his eighties. However, a book that takes his writing as its central matter—and that juxtaposes his writing to the words of Luther, the Hebrew prophets, and Jesus—should probably offer at least the barest sketch of his central concerns and claims. None of these concerns will be expanded upon in this chapter; all will become part of the chapters that follow.

Nature: Central to much of Berry's writing is the effort to get us to think more clearly about what we mean by nature. Too often we mean only that which exists outdoors or is apparently untouched by humans in the wild. Berry writes against such artificial distinctions: humans are a part of the creation, and they shape and are shaped by it whether they wish to be or not.

Economy: Related to Berry's understanding of nature and creation is his conviction that human beings rarely understand economy in its proper sense. Berry speaks of the Great Economy and the Kingdom of God interchangeably; each challenges our smaller human economies to acknowledge their limitations and failures. These first two points—nature and economy—are summarized well by a brief paragraph in "Two Economies":

> . . . the first principle of the Kingdom of God is that it includes everything; in it, the fall of every sparrow is a significant event.

We are in it whether we know it or not and whether we wish to
be or not. Another principle, both ecological and traditional, is
that everything in the Kingdom of God is joined both to it and
to everything else that is in it; that is to say, the Kingdom of God
is orderly. A third principle is that humans do not and can never
know either all the creatures that the Kingdom of God contains or
the whole pattern or order which it contains.[2]

Membership: Several principles follow fairly closely from these observations. First is that membership is not optional. Human beings are
meant for belonging, for participation. Such belonging of course extends
to nature, of which humans are a part; but even more—and especially in
Berry's fiction—such belonging is a chief attribute, even a chief benefit, of
human communities like families and small towns. As the character Burley
Coulter says, "we are members of each other. All of us. Everything. The
difference ain't in who is a member and who is not, but in who knows it
and who don't."[3]

Farming: Berry centers a great deal of his work on the practice, worries, and joys of farming. This concentration is not only because he is a
farmer by background and long experience, but also because he sees our
connection to and care of the land as a measure of health and our discon-
nection from and destruction of the land as a sign of our sickness. To those
who think such concerns rural, rustic, or provincial, Berry is quick to point
out that "eating is an agricultural act,"[4] which is to say, agrarian concerns
are the concern of cities as much as they are the concerns of anywhere else.

Food: Berry's interest in agriculture often centers on the topic of
food—how it is farmed well, why it is so often farmed badly, what it means
to eat well.

Work and pleasure: His focus on farming means that Berry writes
frequently on what constitutes good work and genuine pleasure. He is often
close to despairing when he reflects on the millions of people who do work
they hate in sterile work places. He is equally critical of what most contemporary Americans consider entertainment: Jack Beechum, the admirably
ornery farmer at the center of Berry's strongest novel, reflects Berry's own
disdain "[t]hat a whole roomful of people should sit with their mouths
open like a nest of young birds, peering into a picture box the invariable

2. Berry, *Home Economics*, 55.

3. Berry, *Wild Birds*, 136–37.

4. Berry, *World-Ending Fire*, 144.

message of which is the desirability of Something Else or Someplace Else."[5]
Or, as Berry puts it in one of his poems:

> Shun the electric wire.
> Communicate slowly. Live
> a three-dimensioned life;
> stay away from screens.
> Stay away from anything
> that obscures the place it is in.[6]

Berry is certainly a critic, but we should not conclude from this fact that he is merely saturnine. On the contrary, his stories are routinely jovial, telling of admirable people, rich meals, and gratitude for vocation and community. His poetry and essays as well speak of his gratitude for the life he has been given.

Scale and form: From all that has come so far in this initial sketch, it should not be surprising that Berry is concerned with questions of scale and form, that he is equally willing to praise the small or marginal and to condemn the large and triumphal. His fiction unfolds the blessings of small towns, small farms, and small gestures. His poetry is observational in nature, as are many of his essays. He mistrusts nations and corporations, and he is generally averse to party politics, large-scale movements, and single-issue causes.

Much more can be said; much more will be said. For now, however, we have a fingernail sketch of Berry's central commitments. Further chapters will contextualize these principles through comparison with biblical and theological traditions; indicate how Berry's principles point towards an ecclesial model; and, most importantly, give direction to preachers who wish to engage homiletically in the kind of agrarianism that Berry advocates.

5. Berry, *Memory of Old Jack*, 142.
6. Berry, *New Collected Poems*, 354.

2

Luther's Cross, Berry's Contrariness

THOSE WHO FIND THEMSELVES sympathetic to Berry's basic positions might be tempted to seek a return to some earlier time in the church, whether real or imagined. However, it is neither faithful nor practicable to do so. Rather, the pages that follow will ask how a pastor and preacher can help a congregation to tell itself a story that is truer and more enduring than the very American story of growth, power, and success. Specifically, they will interpret and respond to the various writings of Wendell Berry—essays, stories, and poems—in an effort to answer the following questions: How is a congregation like a farm? How does Berry's understanding of sustainable agrarianism translate into a model for Christian community? Finally, how would such an agrarian ecclesiology provide or at least suggest an agrarian homiletic?

We begin by seeing how Berry's writing, very little of it explicitly theological in its intent, nonetheless finds a toehold among Christian theological traditions. Specifically, there are striking parallels between Luther's theology of the cross and Berry's writing. This probably should not be surprising. Both Berry and Luther express their core commitments in historical settings where multi-national organizations make ever-larger claims for the capaciousness of their domain. Luther challenged a medieval church that in both worldview and financial system ranged across Europe and beyond; Berry's agrarianism is firmly opposed to nation-states, international business, and absentee government oversight. Luther presumed to question established doctrine from the backwater of Wittenberg, Germany; Berry presumes to question a host of modern truisms from the even-greater backwater of rural Kentucky. Both men have a fundamental mistrust for those who presume to transcribe the mysterious or to speak the ineffable; both prefer honest ignorance to dishonest grandstanding. It is hardly surprising, then, that when Luther is highly provocative—as he is in the *Heidelberg Disputation* of 1518—we see strong parallels to Berry.

LUTHER'S THEOLOGY OF THE CROSS

A full explication of Luther's theology of the cross is beyond the scope of this little book, but a few central points can be elucidated. First and foremost, we may say that the central focus of the theology of the cross is God's insistence on working by opposites. We might expect that God would be most clearly manifest in the glorious things in creation and in the church—in sunrises and in cathedrals, in purple mountains and in high attendance numbers. Steve Paulson summarizes this perspective well:

> Glory theologians have a simple rule: if Christ's kingdom has come there will be visible, experiential glory; if it has not come, then there will be suffering. . . . Faith is then correlated with success, victory, and power—if one has true faith, then one succeeds and feels glory.[1]

The theological move Paulson describes here is both deeply human and deeply mistaken. Douglas John Hall labels it "this-worldly triumphalism": "We still want to tell the Christian story as a success story."[2] For Luther, it is the worst kind of theology: "That person does not deserve to be called a theologian who perceives the invisible things of God as understandable on the basis of those things which have been made."[3] Rather than inquiring of God where God is to be found, we take our own sinful and egoistical assumptions and place them upon God. Surely, we are tempted to think, if God can be understood as infinitely large and powerful, then God's fingerprints are most visible among the successful and powerful of the world. Luther insists that this approach is fundamentally wrong, that we are most benighted when we claim to see God where God has not chosen to be revealed.

1. Paulson, *Lutheran Theology*, 142.
2. Hall, *End of Christendom and the Future of Christianity*, 21.
3. Luther, *Annotated Luther*, 1:83.

Where ought we to look then? Timothy Wengert gives a succinct answer to this question in his shorthand summary of Luther's *theologia crucis*: "the realization, the *revelatio sub contrario specie*, of our true neediness . . . . This is Luther's traditional definition of the theology of the cross; it is finding God in the last place we would reasonably look."[4] We are to look, in other words, where our deepest need drives us to look rather than where we would like to look. Our need drives us to Christ, and this means turning to the cross: "The person deserves to be called a theologian, however, who understands the visible and the 'backside' of God [Exod. 33:23] seen through suffering and the cross."[5] There is a lot going on here. First, the visible things of the world are no longer a means to an end: we do not presume to see God by analogy to the world. Second, we look for God where God has chosen to be revealed—in the cross and, by extension, in suffering generally. Third, the cross becomes the lens by which we understand the world and God's role in it: we not only look to the cross; we look through it. Finally, we do not presume to look behind or beyond the cross.

Much follows from this, starting with the basic realization that God and the ways of God are often deeply shocking to us. Despite our best efforts, we continue to conflate the ways of God with the ways of the world, and so God's activity often eludes us and then catches us off-guard. For sure this is the constant witness of Scripture. God's chosen people are a heterogeneous set of tribes, not a great empire. The signal victory of God is a retreat across a seabed, not a glorious conquest. God's seers and prophets routinely speak truth to power, confronting royal prerogatives more often than confirming them. God's messiah is born in Bethlehem, not Jerusalem; laid in a manger somewhere out of doors, not in a palace. This messiah's mighty deeds are not military, political, or economic by any ordinary measure; they are most frequently healings, exorcisms, and feedings performed for people of no worldly account. His teachings are routinely parabolic and cryptic, and they emphasize a discipleship of endurance and suffering. His so-called theophany is a Roman execution followed by a resurrection that is witnessed by precisely nobody. Is this any way to save the world?

The theologian of the cross answers with an unequivocal Yes. It is not how humanity would have thought to save the world, but, then again, we are the ones who got the world into the mess it is in. Once this shocking affirmation begins to settle in, then God's presence can be affirmed in the

4. Wengert in "Special Issue," 205.

5. Luther, *Annotated Luther,* 1:83.

most surprising places: in an infant or a penitent adult forgiven and welcomed by water and the word; in bread and wine as Christ present among the people; in God's word spoken through fallible human words; in feeding the hungry and repenting for gluttony; in housing the homeless and repenting for greed; in caring for the least and the lost and the lonely. Even when programs and organizations grow larger, the genuine theologian of the cross will see God at work not in terms of scale but in terms of the encounters, rescues, and relationships where God is making a difference.

All of this is profoundly disturbing to human reason. Indeed, part of what made Luther's exposition of the theology of the cross so troubling in his own time is that it upset the apple cart of medieval hierarchies. C. S. Lewis has pointed out that the great strength of the Middle Ages was synthesis: "At his most characteristic, medieval man . . . was an organizer, a codifier, a builder of systems. . . . The perfect examples are the *Summa* of Aquinas and Dante's *Divine Comedy*; as unified and ordered as the Parthenon . . . "[6] Systematic works such as these express belief in a cosmos that is in many ways accessible to the rational mind. Into such a world as that, an insistence that most hierarchical analogies are mistaken—that they are in fact reason going where it ought not go and claiming what it cannot possibly know—is a lightning strike. Indeed, to this day the most radical elements of Luther's theology of the cross trouble devout Christians when they first encounter them. What, for example, is the typical layperson to do with a claim that the "works of the righteous would be mortal sins were they not feared as mortal sins by the righteous themselves out of pious fear of God"?[7]

One of the other significant consequences of the theology of the cross is that it plays havoc with our understanding and use of scale. It seems to me that there is nothing more common among Christians than a desire to see their faith in God validated in larger congregations, more popular programs and ministries, and more money as a bulwark against the future. These are all examples of a theology of glory, of believing that God is not only impressed by grandeur but is actually reflected in it. The theology of the cross, though, says precisely the opposite: success, size, and prosperity are worldly measures and do not reflect the God revealed on Calvary. On the contrary, God is to be found in the small and the particular: in suffering

---

6. Lewis, *Discarded Image*, 10.
7. Luther, *Annotated Luther*, 1:82.

and in empathy, in faithfulness and endurance, in the gift of food, in genuine community.

There is more that could be said about the theology of the cross, but even in this brief overview we find four central methods or patterns that are equally at home in Wendell Berry's writing: seeing by opposites, openness to surprise, a willingness to trouble mere reason, and a recalibration of scale.

LEARNING FROM BERRY'S MAD FARMER

As has already been noted, Berry is not a theologian by training. However, that fact should not blind us to the way his agrarian perspective echoes the theology of the cross. For Berry land and the care of the land are fundamental lenses. As he writes, "I take literally the statement in the Gospel of John that God loves the world. I believe the world was created and approved by love, that it subsists, coheres, and endures by love, and that, insofar as it is redeemable, it can be redeemed only by love."[8] For many of us, such a reference to John 3 would not be an agrarian claim, but for Berry it doubtless is. "The world" is not abstract, and it is not something that can be visually summarized by a photograph of the earth taken from space or even by a photograph of a galaxy. It is instead ten thousand individual places, all of them loved by God. As Berry goes on to write, "I believe that divine love, incarnate and indwelling in the world, summons the world always toward wholeness."[9]

Berry's version of opposites is contrariness: even as the theologian of the cross sees God where we would not reasonably think to look, Berry encourages us to be contrary, i.e., to speak and act against the grain of a triumphalist culture. This approach is especially evident in the set of poems he has written referred to as the "mad farmer" poems. Among these "The Contrariness of the Mad Farmer" sets Berry most clearly at odds with both a cultural and an ecclesiastical theology of glory. The poem begins thus:

> I am done with apologies. If contrariness is my
> inheritance and destiny, so be it. If it is my mission
> to go in at exits and come out at entrances, so be it.[10]

8. Berry, *Another Turn of the Crank*, 89.

9. Berry, *Another Turn of the Crank*, 89.

10. Berry, *New Collected Poems*, 139.

The mad farmer then describes himself as one who has "planted by the stars in defiance of the experts" and "tilled somewhat by incantation and by singing."[11] We see here the posture of one who sets himself against the prevailing fondness for size and worldly success, against monoculture farms and a society that eats but does not believe that good farming matters. The position he stands against is made clear in the opening lines of another mad farmer poem, "Manifesto: The Mad Farmer Liberation Front":

> Love the quick profit, the annual raise,
> vacation with pay. Want more
> of everything ready-made. Be afraid
> to know your neighbors and to die.[12]

There is a pain in the sarcasm of these lines, the recognition that success and glory are shallow, that they lead to anxiety and fear, and that they are nonetheless highly prized.

The contrariness of the mad farmer, on the other hand, is discontent with such shallow aspirations and seeks to open our eyes to uncomfortable truths; like Luther's cross, it takes us where we do not want to go. Berry is willing to make us uncomfortable because he believes that the mad farmer is aware of gifts that are genuine and enduring. As Berry writes in the "Author's Note" to *The Mad Farmer Poems*,

> The joke of the Mad Farmer Poems is that in a society gone insane
> with industrial greed & insecurity, a man exuberantly sane will
> appear to be 'mad'. . . . These poems. . . . embody a vision of san-
> ity breaking forth into a world driven crazy by dreams of wealth,
> power, and ease—and so by fear.[13]

The person who is willing to look at the world as it truly is will appear to be mad, while the insanity of the world insists that it is sane even in the face of its own absurdity.

Berry's contrariness is not only similar to Luther's theology of the cross by way of analogy. In other words, Berry does not have an approach to agrarianism that is accidentally similar to Luther or that is similar but employed to unrelated purposes. On the contrary, Berry believes that contrariness has much to do with a proper perspective on God. Thus "The Contrariness of the Mad Farmer" contains an extended jeremiad against

11. Berry, *New Collected Poems,* 139.

12. Berry, *New Collected Poems*, 173.

13. Berry, *Mad Farmer Poems*, v.

Christendom and an implicit praise of a God who is known in the surprising and in the local:

> "Pray," they said, and I laughed, covering myself
> in the earth's brightness, and then stole off gray
> into the midst of a revel, and prayed like an orphan.
> When they said, "I know that my Redeemer liveth,"
> I told them, "He's dead," and when they told me,
> "God is dead," I answered, "He goes fishing every day
> in the Kentucky River. I see Him often."[14]

Those against whom the mad farmer protests are both the church—those who tell people to pray and who sing hymns—and also the academy, scholars such as those found in the "God is dead" movement. The farmer's counter-assertions are both genuine and faithful, but they can only be seen by someone looking from below—the one "Going against men" and "having heard at times a deep harmony / thrumming in the mixture."[15]

The mad farmer's perspective, then, is deeply congenial to the element of surprise that is so central to Luther's theology of the cross. Its measure is the land—the world as the object of God's particular love—and as such it is constantly surprised and frequently delighted. Even as the theologian of the cross comes to rejoice in the suffering and death by which God rescues a people, so the agrarian following Berry's lead rejoices in the seasons and their cycle of life, death, and new life.

And just as Luther's theology of the cross surprised and offended the theologies of glory rampant in his day, so Berry's agrarianism is a surprise and an offense to moderns who have embraced the hermeneutic of progress and expansion so central to our technologically obsessed age. Perhaps no essay of Berry's so clearly illustrates both the surprising nature of his perspective and the stridency of those who disagree with him as the brief essay "Why I Am Not Going to Buy a Computer" from 1987. In three short pages Berry advances a straightforward argument. First, using a computer to write is a disrupting alternative to the local economy that he and his wife have developed: it would diminish his connection to the place in which he writes and about which he writes, and it would replace her as his editor and typist and critic. As he writes, "what would be superseded would be not only something, but somebody."[16] Second, he would also place himself

14. Berry, *New Collected Poems*, 139.

15. Berry, *New Collected Poems*, 139.

16. Berry, *What Are People For?*, 171.

increasingly in debt to energy companies and computer companies who do not care—as he does—about the health of the world in which we live. And finally, buying a computer constitutes assenting to a form of triumphalism: "I do not wish to fool myself. I disbelieve, and therefore strongly resent, the assertion that I or anybody else could write better or more easily with a computer than with a pencil."[17] This stance offends a dozen contemporary sensibilities about how technology improves our daily lives, about how large corporations—but not consumers—are to blame for ecological damage, and about our own role in the march of progress.

That Berry was surprising and offending many of his readers became clear in the responses they gave when the article was first published in *Harper's*. Indeed, their responses make clear that agrarianism, like Luther's theology of the cross, is troubling to reason, especially reason in the service of "progress." They accused him of misogyny: "Wendell Berry provides writers enslaved by the computer with a handy alternative: Wife—a low-tech energy-saving device."[18] They imply that he is naïve and that the problem is with someone else: "I would be happy to join Berry in a protest against strip mining, but I intend to keep plugging this computer into the wall with a clear conscience."[19] Finally, they engage in arguments that are largely *ad hominem*, pointing out that his article is published in a magazine that carries ad for the companies he eschews: "If Berry rests comfortably at night, he must be using sleeping pills."[20] Berry offers an extended response to all of these, but the point here is not to adjudicate the issue but to recognize the pattern. Contrarianism, like the theology of the cross, is almost always a minority voice, a prophetic voice unheeded in royal halls. The reaction it garners, however, is routinely disproportionate. Its claim that triumphalism and glory are hollow and ultimately self-destructive must perforce be met with force. No one may be permitted to demur from the modern myths of wealth, power, and progress by means of new technologies.

Finally, we see overlap between Luther and Berry when we address ourselves to questions of scale. Even as Luther's theology challenges a mentality that glories in pomp, hierarchy, and the ecclesiastical economy of his day, so Berry's agrarianism challenges the corporations, policies, and practices that protect contemporary triumphalism. Berry's love for small

17. Berry, *What Are People For?*, 171.

18. Berry, *What Are People For?*, 172.

19. Berry, *What Are People For?*, 173.

20. Berry, *What Are People For?*, 175.

farms and his disdain for large-scale farming (or "agri-business") are probably the place where questions of scale come to the fore most often in his
writing. In family farming one sees the preservation of families and communities, of customs and traditional knowledge, and of care for the land.
In agri-business one sees the opposite: individuals are pressed by financial
necessity to go elsewhere for work, families forced to "[g]et big or get out.
Sell out and go to town"[21]; the land then is treated as a mere resource that
can be exploited by machinery and chemicals. A vivid example of what
Berry espouses and opposes is revealed in his use of a brief news story. He
quotes an article from *Christian Century* in which a young man who works
for a large swine farm is fired for taking the time and effort to heal several
diseased swine rather than slaughter them as was policy. Berry writes:

> The young worker in the hog factory is a direct cultural descendant
> of the shepherd in the parable, just about opposite and perhaps
> incomprehensible to the "practical" rationalist. But the practical
> implications are still the same. Would you rather have your pigs
> cared for by a young man who had compassion for them or by
> one who would indifferently knock them in the head? Which of
> the two would be more likely to prevent disease in the first place?
> Compassion, of course, is the crux of the issue. For "company pol-
> icy" must exclude compassion; if compassion were to be admitted
> to consideration, such a "farm" could not exist.[22]

Berry's comparison of the young man—who represents the knowledge and skill of the small-farm mentality—to the shepherd who leaves
the ninety-nine to save the one clarifies why scale matters. As he writes:
"Compassion is the crux of the issue." Small-scale farming gives a greater
opportunity to recognize the manifold factors that the large-scale mind literally cannot afford to consider, factors like human obligations to creation
and to fellow creatures.

Berry's interpretation of the story of the young man who cared for
sick pigs is certainly useful for considering scale; for our present purposes it
also serves a larger role. Like the parable of the shepherd and his lost sheep,
this parabolic story exemplifies the various points of contact between Luther's cruciformity and Berry's agrarian contrariness. Both the shepherd
and the man who cared for pigs are oppositional or contrary in the way
they understand moral and economic values. For each of them there is a

21. Berry, *Bringing It to the Table*, 74.
22. Berry, *Citizenship Papers*, 94–95.

consideration that is larger than personal security. They are thus surprising and even scandalous figures. Commentators and preachers routinely point out the shock of the shepherd who leaves behind the ninety-nine, even as one might be shocked by the woman who throws a party because she has found a single coin, or as one might be shocked by a father who throws good money after bad, slaughtering the fatted calf when his no-account son shows up at his door. So too the young man scandalizes the management of the pig farm. He is an offense to reason: who worries about a one-percent loss in flock size; who risks a job to save a few sick pigs? In all these ways we see how Luther and Berry are especially responsive to the gospel as that which proclaims and enacts an overturning of our worldly concerns and commitments.

3

Scripture, the Land, and the Agrarian Community

THE BIBLICAL WORK THAT undergirds this book and engages in dialogue with Berry comes from scriptural understandings of land, economy, and community. Specifically, it looks at how both the Old and New Testaments understand the gift of land and the commitments of an agrarian economy in relationship to the community of faith. These concerns will take different shapes in the two testaments. The land is, simply put, a literal gift in the Hebrew Scriptures in a way that it rarely is in the uniquely Christian books; further, the Old Testament—and especially the Old Testament prophets— place economic questions front and center in a way that is often more explicit than in the New Testament. This book, then, will follow the lead of Berry, Ellen Davis, and others by looking first at how the Old Testament writers understand the land.

OLD TESTAMENT

The issue of the Old Testament's understanding of land and agrarianism is so vast that its full exposition is beyond the scope of these pages. Fortunately, Ellen Davis has written a book on precisely this topic: *Scripture, Culture, and Agriculture: An Agrarian Reading of the Bible*. Davis has recognized before most others that Berry and other agrarians bring with them an approach to Scripture that is capacious and vital. As she writes, agrarianism is inevitably central to a correct understanding of Scripture: "The fact that land possession is a central (arguably *the* central) issue of the Hebrew Scriptures thus confirms their fundamentally agrarian character."[1] This is true first and foremost in the creation story of Genesis 2, a story in which God bears a striking resemblance to a farmer: bringing life from the dirt, creating orchards, forming beasts in relationship to the humans who name them, instructing his stewards to till the land. Davis concurs with such a reading:

> from a biblical perspective, farming is the primary human vocation, 'serving and preserving' the fertile earth (Gen. 2:15). . . . As many passages attest, the land itself is the medium or even the agent through which we may experience life as divinely blessed, or conversely, accursed (Gen. 3:17; 4:11; Leviticus 26; Psalms 72; 37).[2]

Davis drives the point home by reminding the reader of the etymological connection between human and earth in the Hebrew: "a fundament of biblical anthropology, as set forth in the first chapters of Genesis, is that there is a kinship between humans and the earth: 'And YHWH God formed the human being [*adam*], dust from the fertile soil [*adama*]' (Gen. 2:7)."[3]

Examples for the centrality of land, land possession, and land management in Scripture could be multiplied almost beyond count. Much of Genesis could be fairly described as the promise of land followed by the vagaries of coming into possession of it. Exodus, the rest of the Pentateuch, and Judges are largely concerned with return to the land, possession of the land, and proper use of the land. Ezra and Nehemiah have at their center the return to the land; and on and on. This is not to say that there are no other central biblical themes; it is to say that any effort to read the Hebrew Scriptures faithfully that does not address agrarian issues is doomed to be partial and distorted at best.

At this point we must be cautious, willing to acknowledge that simply pointing to God's gift of land and its centrality does not constitute a comprehensive agrarian claim. For the Scriptures are concerned not simply with grateful reception of the land but also with the proper use of it. That is to say, they are concerned with the economic issues attendant upon the land. The law as found in the Pentateuch certainly addresses economic issues. Even more valuable for this study is the witness of the prophets.

1. Davis, *Scripture, Culture, and Agriculture*, 101.
2. Davis, *Scripture, Culture, and Agriculture*, 104.
3. Davis, *Scripture, Culture, and Agriculture*, 29.

Not all the prophets make central the economic issues of the land, and—even if they did—we could not address every one of them here. Nonetheless, it is worth noting that the four great eighth-century prophets—Isaiah, Hosea, Amos, and Micah—all reflect this concern. They do so in different ways and to differing degrees, but their consensus that land and land economy are crucial to the call of God's people to be faithful indicates fairly conclusively that the land is not a one-time gift to be used however the nation sees fit but rather an ongoing gift, promise, and covenant. Such a gift calls for the people to engage in faithfulness towards God and justice towards one another and towards the land itself.

It must be acknowledged that First Isaiah has other emphases than the land at its core; its focus on Zion and on the Davidic line means that its locus of thought and speech is often urban and centered on the temple. The first chapter complains of "your new moons and your appointed festivals [that] my soul hates" (1:14) and laments how "the faithful city has become a whore" (1:21). Nonetheless, Isaiah certainly knows the economic connection between city and country: he can lament "the vines of Sibmah, whose clusters once made drunk the lords of the nations, reached to Jazer and strayed to the desert" (16:8). Like other pre-industrial peoples, he is daily aware that the city draws its life from the food produced in the countryside.

First Isaiah's awareness of this relationship becomes especially clear when he speaks of judgment and the possibility of redemption, for in such places he frequently employs agricultural or natural metaphors. Thus, when "the LORD is about to lay waste the earth and make it desolate," this image of a scorched earth has economic roots and economic consequences: "as with the buyer, so with the seller; as with the lender, so with the borrower. . . . The earth shall be laid waste and utterly despoiled" (24:1–3). Again, when Isaiah speaks of eschatological rescue, the earth itself is central to the story: "he will destroy on this mountain the shroud that is cast over all peoples . . . he will swallow up death forever" (25:7). It is not going too far to say that people and earth are to be saved in one, single act of salvation: "the disgrace of his people he will take away from all the earth . . . let us be glad and rejoice in his salvation" (25:8–9).

Isaiah does not connect God's justice and humanity's economic injustice as frequently or as explicitly as Amos and Micah, and yet it bears noticing that in one of the most evocative passages in Isaiah—the song or parable of the unfruitful vineyard—this is precisely the connection Isaiah makes. The elements of the song build in ways that are initially straightforward.

God's people are seen as a vineyard: "the vineyard of the LORD is the house of Israel, and the people of Judah are his pleasant planting" (5:7). God gives them the land and builds a watchtower—images of covenant and of protection. The threat of the vineyard being torn down and trampled is a powerful metaphor for defeat in war and for exile. Further, given Isaiah's emphasis on fidelity to the Holy One of Israel, YHWH, it would not be unreasonable to suspect that the wild grapes of the song represent foreign practices and gods. And yet, when Isaiah declares that God "expected justice, but saw bloodshed," the central matter for him is not faithful worship but just economic practices: "Ah, you who join house to house, who add field to field, until there is room for no one but you, and you are left to live alone in the midst of the land" (5:8–9). Nor does the prophet stop there; the metaphorical exile of the song is made explicit: "The LORD of hosts has sworn it in my hearing: Surely many houses shall be desolate, large and beautiful homes, without inhabitant" (5:9). The language is explicit and surprisingly contemporary: God is angered by those who do not respect the boundaries of family farms and who devastate local communities. The punishment will fit the offense: the housing bubble will collapse, and those who have built their wealth on rotten economic principles will be removed from the land.

Hosea's emphasis is similar to Isaiah's, though in some ways more pointed: his indictments against Israel are rooted in the people's failure to recognize or remember that the blessings of earth and harvest are a gift of YHWH and not of the Baals. In other words, infidelity to YHWH is reflected in misuse of the land and its gifts:

> [Israel] did not know
> that it was I who gave her
> the grain, the wine, and the oil,
> and who lavished upon her silver
> and gold that they used for Baal.
> Therefore I will take back
> my grain in its time
> and my wine in its season;
> and I will take away my wool and my flax,
> which were to cover her nakedness. (2:8–9)

In short, Hosea declares, Israel does not suffer alone for her infidelity: the land itself is harmed.

> Hear the word of the LORD, O people of Israel;
> for the LORD has an indictment against the inhabitants of the land.

> There is no faithfulness or loyalty,
>   and no knowledge of God in the land. . . .
> Therefore the land mourns,
>   and all who live in it languish;
> together with the wild animals
>   and the birds of the air,
>   even the fish of the sea are perishing. (4:1–2,4)

It would be eisegesis to claim that Hosea is foretelling our contemporary misuse of the planet; it is not inappropriate, however, to claim that Hosea stands firmly in the biblical tradition that asserts that human beings are central to God's creation and that their failures are reflected in the world around them. When Israel chases after other gods—when humanity seeks a human economy that is at odds with God's greater economy—the earth suffers and "the land mourns."

Amos is concerned broadly with the way the rich take advantage of the poor: "For three transgressions of Israel, and for four, I will not revoke the punishment; because they sell the righteous for silver, and the needy for a pair of sandals" (2:6). The parallel poetic structure that links "the righteous" and "the needy" is a prophetic staple that will continue to see expression as far into Israel's history as the teachings of Jesus of Nazareth. Amos further sees the well-being of the land adversely affected by the greed of the rich: "I also withheld the rain from you when there were still three months to the harvest. . . . I struck you with blight and mildew. . . . the locust devoured your fig trees and your olive trees; yet you did not return to me, says the LORD" (4:7–9). Finally, like Isaiah Amos sees the land in sympathetic relationship to God's people: "Shall not the land tremble on this account, and everyone mourn who lives in it, and all of it rise like the Nile?" (8:8).

Isaiah, Hosea, and Amos see vital connections between heaven and earth, between the covenant and the economy, and between fidelity to YHWH and justice to one's neighbors. Yet if we want to observe the prophet for whom worship of YHWH and agrarian economics are of central and overwhelming concern, we must turn to Micah. Micah is the prophet who most clearly has a special concern for the ways in which poverty is connected to farming and to rural existence.

A few brief passages give a clear sense of how Micah views the relationship among land, economic justice, and the covenant. It would not be strong enough to say that economic injustice is a result of faithlessness to the covenant (as we might, for example, with Isaiah). No, for Micah the injustice is faithlessness itself. Exploitation of the people and the land is no mere sign that the covenant has been violated; it is itself the violation. Thus, as Micah turns from the doom that will come upon the cities of Judah to the causes of that doom, the lamentation begins "Alas for those who devise wickedness and evil deeds on their bed" and continues immediately to "They covet fields, and seize them; houses, and take them away; they oppress householder and house, people and their inheritance" (2:1–2). It is no accident that this claim of land seizure by the powerful is central to the complaint of Berry and other agrarians: as Micah makes clear, severing people from a sustainable relationship to their land has always been a money-maker for outsiders who wish to profit from but not live in agrarian communities.

The punishment from the LORD for these transgressions is precise: you will "wail with bitter lamentation, and say, 'We are utterly ruined; the LORD alters the inheritance of my people. . . . Among our captors he parcels out the fields'" (2:4). This punishment goes to the heart of God's covenant with Israel: their misuse of the land God has given will result in their enemies taking promised land away from them. Nor is this the only passage in which God's response is literally grounded in the land itself. The covenant lawsuit between God and the people of the land takes up the first half of chapter 6, and it begins with the land itself being called to play the role of witness: "Rise, plead your case before the mountains, and let the hills hear your voice. Hear, you mountains, the controversy of the LORD, and you enduring foundations of the earth" (6:1–2). The setting and the stakes could not be higher for Micah: all the earth is called to be a witness to the economic injustices inflicted by God's people through their corrupt use of the land.

Much more could be said. At this point, however, it seems unremarkable to claim that land is at the heart of the Hebrew Scriptures, that the land is an ongoing sign of the covenant, that justice in land usage is an economic necessity placed upon Israel, and that Israel's frequent failure to deal justly with the people and the land is a profound sign of faithlessness before YHWH.

NEW TESTAMENT

The New Testament's relationship to land and community is a varied and complex topic. It would be shallow scholarship that tried in this short space to summarize, let alone synthesize, an issue so vast that it encompasses the implied communities of the Gospel writers, the various congregations founded by or in ongoing relationship with Paul, the ecclesiology and ethics of the later letters, the theology of heaven and earth found in Revelation, and much more. More valuable, and more pertinent to Berry's own writing, is to focus on the ways Jesus talks about land and community. Specifically, what do his teaching and actions with an agrarian focus tell us about how Jesus understands questions of land, place, and community?

The first point to be made is that, in a basic or fundamental sense, nearly all of Jesus' ministry is amenable to an agrarian reading. His ministry occurs largely out of doors and almost entirely with people who are deeply connected to the land and to each other—members of families and small towns, farmers, fishermen, those gathering at village synagogues or out in the wilderness to hear him preach. Beyond that, of course, he also devotes much of his time to ministry among those who are marginal by cultural design—women, widows, children, the poor, the paralyzed, the blind, the deaf, demoniacs. In short, even a cursory review of the Gospels makes a *prima facie* case that the central tenets of agrarianism—economic focus on the small and local and a concomitant suspicion of power and glory, to name just two—find fertile ground in the ministry of Jesus.

What is more, it is not infrequently that those who oppose Jesus or those who are brought to radical conversion by him have implicitly been living counter to an agrarian perspective: such people are routinely associated with large cities like Jerusalem or distant empires like Rome—tax collectors such as Levi (Mark 2:14), chief priests, Roman governors, and Sadducees. Those who disdain or judge him routinely do so in language that evokes a theology of glory: "Can anything good come out of Nazareth?" (John 1:46); "Do you not know that I have power to release you, and power to crucify you?" (John 19:10); "You who would destroy the temple and build it in three days, save yourself, and come down from the cross!" (Mark 15:29). Even Pharisees, representatives of a lay movement focusing on people in everyday life, become the exception that proves the rule: their apparent victory over Jesus comes when they join forces with urban and imperial powers to whom they are otherwise antagonistic.

When we look for particular deeds and teachings that focus on agrarian issues, we find them not occasionally or sporadically but regularly. Jesus turns repeatedly to the land as a resource for his ministry. So, for example, the wedding at Cana in John 2 comes into a particular kind of clarity when we view it in an agrarian light. It is not merely that this is a sign which has at its center agricultural elements—water, grapes, wine—but that through this sign Jesus is a hidden revelation, a revelation unrecognizable to the theologian of glory or triumphalism. No one knows how the water is transformed, of course, but the mystery does not stop there: the so-called central figures, the bridegroom and the steward, have no idea that anything especially unusual has occurred other than the order in which the good wine is served. It is the marginal figures who see and believe—the servants and the disciples (and even they grasp precious little about who this mysterious figure is).

Many of the other mighty deeds and signs share this same double pattern, namely, natural or agricultural elements combined with Jesus as a hidden revelation of God. In the Synoptic Gospels he calms the storm, causing his disciples to wonder aloud, "Who then is this, that even the wind and the sea obey him?" (Mark 4:41). On more than one occasion he feeds a multitude of people from just a few loaves and fishes. Where the theologian of glory will emphasize the numbers fed, a theologian of the cross in an agrarian mode will emphasize the indirection of the event, the way in which—much like the wedding at Cana—many receive the benefit of the mighty deed but few understand its origin or what it says about Jesus. In short, the mighty deeds routinely call a theologian of the cross or an agrarian reader of the Gospels to notice that Jesus' actions do not aim—as is so often assumed—to point to his heavenly origin but rather to reveal the surprising ways that heaven and earth meet in the Messiah.

John's Gospel regularly provides us with this type of double insight— agricultural language combined with Jesus as a hidden revelation. John's method is different, of course. The Synoptic Gospels "hide Jesus" by what might be called a disinclination to over-explain. Scenes are generally brief; teachings—especially parables and apocalyptic prophecy—are rarely explained or clarified; Jesus speaks of himself indirectly and even equivocally ("you say that I am"). John however goes in an entirely different direction, hiding Jesus in plain sight. Scenes in John are long, even protracted. Teachings are extensive, gathering nuance by means of repetition and variation. Most importantly, Jesus speaks of himself directly and unequivocally. A clear example of these elements is the "I am" statements. They are rooted for the most part in extended passages that offer profound and complex claims about the nature of Jesus. Nevertheless Jesus is hidden in such passages—hidden not by the indirection of his language but by the incapacity of the hearers to recognize the direction in which the language points.

The significance of the "I am" passages in John has long been recognized. Perhaps less obvious is that, of the traditional seven "I am" statements, five of them trade in explicitly agricultural and creation metaphors: bread (6:35), light[4] (8:12; 9:5), gate for the sheep (10:7), good shepherd (10:11, 14), and true vine (15:1). It is not going too far to say that John presents Jesus as a figure deeply tied to God's creation and especially to the life of the land. Of critical importance is the lens by which the theologian or preacher interprets these metaphors. A theologian of glory or someone tied to a triumphalist reading of John as the "spiritual" Gospel[5] will be inclined to see each metaphor as mere husk containing or even hiding the real or actual meaning. In such readings, bread and wine become unequivocally sacramental; light becomes enlightenment or theophany or the gift of salvation; the gate and the good shepherd become figures in a preexisting drama about "being saved" and "going to heaven." None of these readings is fully wrong: of course bread and wine are ultimately sacramental; of course light betokens glory; of course Jesus is speaking towards ultimate things when he speaks of himself as a herder of sheep.

However, the theologian of the cross and the mad farmer ask us to slow down and to dwell in the presence of the metaphor as fully as possible before presuming to interpret it. It seems to matter to Jesus and to John that we see the Galilean not as a speaker of timeless truth but as the word of God spoken within the agrarian world of his time. An agrarian reader wants to recognize that bread and wine are two of the most basic products of the first-century farm: they are the absolute building blocks of subsistence farming and survival. An agrarian reader pauses to remember how few the sources of light were in the first century—how much the sun and the moon and the stars mattered—and therefore the extent to which knowledge of light was crucial to understanding seasons, tending of crops,

4. By using our imaginations just a bit, we can also realize that Jesus' conversation with the Samaritan woman includes the claim "I am" (4:26) and the claim to give "a spring of water gushing up to eternal life" (4:14).To be the source of water and light is, from an agrarian point of view, awfully close to Jesus as life itself; and life is at the center of the final two "I am" statements: resurrection and life (11:25) and way and truth and life (14:6).

5. As Karoline Lewis makes clear in her *John* (Fortress Biblical Preaching Commentaries), this view of John as more "spiritual" than the other Gospels has a long history, one that goes back at least as far as Clement of Alexandria. Thankfully, there has been resistance to this in recent scholarship. Perhaps no one has addressed the issue more directly than Lewis herself, who makes challenging the old consensus the first issue she tackles in the Introduction to her John commentary.

and the care of animals. An agrarian reader and a theologian of the cross realize that, before anything else, Jesus as gate and shepherd and vine are rural metaphors, metaphors that tie him to the land as much as they tie him to Old Testament ideas about kingship.

There are other explicitly agrarian teachings that occur outside of the parables, but only a few can be highlighted in this limited space. Among the most significant is an apparently minor conversation between Jesus and his disciples: "When he saw the crowds, he had compassion for them, because they were like sheep without a shepherd. Then he said to his disciples, 'The harvest is plentiful, but the laborers are few; therefore ask the Lord of the harvest to send out laborers into his harvest'" (Matt 9:36–37). The theologian of glory is likely to understand such a passage in terms of church growth or the richness of the evangelism field. An agrarian theologian is likely to notice two things instead. First, as is so often the case, Jesus chooses to speak of the kingdom of God in agricultural terms. And while harvest as metaphor certainly indicates an opportunity for human beings to work in the fields of the Lord and reap plenitude to God's glory, it is not something reducible to mechanical process. It is not a conveyor belt or an investment portfolio or a website selling products. Unlike these, there is an irreducible element of mystery to the harvest: it is where the gifts of the creation and the labor of mortals bring forth new life. What it calls from the laborers is not greed or glory or rapaciousness but fidelity and labor; the faithful laborer is a disciple and a farmer.

Second, an agrarian theologian will notice the title given to God here: Lord of the Harvest (*kyrios tou therismou*). God in such a metaphor is many things, few of them useful to theologians of glory: creator, giver of sun and rain and seasons, farmer, reaper, sower, and others. In this title God is remarkable for the fidelity and labor that God brings to the task of shepherding the people.

The picture painted thus far is of an agrarianism that shows itself scattered across the four Gospels, available to be seen in many of the mighty deeds and signs, in the "I am" statements of John, and in more than a few of the teachings found in the Synoptic Gospels. What is left to review is the largest trove of agrarian teachings in the Gospels, namely the parables. They have not been left for last simply because of their prominence; they have also been left for last because the connection they make between the land and creation on one hand and the economic aspects of the gospel on the other places them at the center of agrarian concerns.

Numbers do not tell the whole story, but it is worth noting the sheer volume of parables that work within an agricultural or rural milieu: the workers in the vineyard, the lost sheep, the sower and the seed, the barren fig tree, the seed growing secretly, the weeds and the wheat, the mustard seed, the net and the fish, the wheat and the leaven, the treasure in the field, the pearl of great price, the laborers in the vineyard, the two sons. Several others might be included,[6] especially those about feasting, but even such a list as this makes clear that the parables of Jesus bear more than a passing relationship to agriculture and agrarianism.

It might be tempting to think of such a claim as common sense (how else would a rabbi from Galilee of the gentiles construct his teachings?), but such an instinct is both condescending and narrow. After all, there are plenty of other areas of human knowledge that Jesus could have used or used more frequently than he did: palaces and the life of royalty, international politics, travel, the sea, wild animals, signs in the heavens, warfare, clothing and jewelry, and on and on. Such vast fields make occasional appearances in the parables—the king going to war, a traveling Samaritan— but these pale in comparison to the wealth of farmers, managers, stewards, tenants, workers, fields, vineyards, trees, wheat, leaven, seeds, pearls, and others that populate Jesus' parables. He presents himself in the four Gospels as a teacher aware of the kind of agriculturally centered life his listeners live and also of the fecundity of the images and metaphors available to him within those settings.

Most parables are open to a range of interpretations, even those closest to allegory; and thus the agricultural parables of Jesus do not permit of a single meaning or even a narrow range of shared meanings. However, there are overlapping themes and interests; and three of these parables draw out this overlap quite clearly: the workers in the vineyard (Matt 20:1–16), the lost sheep (Luke 15:3–7),[7] the sower and the seed (Mark 4:1–20).[8] In each of these parables there is an element of surprise and even scandal, and the theologian of the cross will recognize this element as hidden revelation or as a divine foolishness that is wiser than mortal wisdom. What is more, the surprise or scandal is economic, and the parables point to an economic worldview that is as large as the kingdom of God and as particular as a

6. The prodigal son or lost son in particular might also be added to this list: issues of famine, animal husbandry, farming, and feasting are all present.

7. Cf. Matt 18:12–14.

8. Cf. Matt 13:3–23 and Luke 8:5–15.

worker, a sheep, and a seed. It is, in other words, an economy wildly at variance with glory and with triumphalism.

The parable of the lost sheep is a good place to begin because it indicates well how easy it is to underread a parable. Someone skimming the parable quickly will glean correctly that the parable tells us how much Christ values his children and rejoices when they are found: "Just so, I tell you, there will be more joy in heaven over one sinner who repents than over ninety-nine righteous people who need no repentance" (Luke 15:7). But there is so much more. Someone attentive to Luther's theology of the cross will note the shocking aspect of the parable—that the shepherd has to leave the ninety-nine and risk going into the wilderness to retrieve the one who has been lost. The agrarian will add that such a risk would never be taken by someone with an economy focused on numbers, growth, and success. Only a shepherd who cares about the animal—who sees the relationship between sheep, shepherd, and flock in terms of God's economy—would risk so much for so little in the way of material return.

Berry distinguishes between these two approaches to the lost sheep by speaking of a Rational Mind versus a Sympathetic Mind. He notes that "The rationalist, we may be sure, has a hundred sheep because he has a plan for that many. The one who has gone astray has escaped not only from the flock but also from the plan. . . . Wouldn't it be best to consider the lost sheep a 'trade-off' for the safety of the ninety-nine?"[9] On the other hand, Berry asserts, the shepherd is in a very different position:

> the shepherd is a shepherd because he embodies the Sympathetic Mind. Because he is a man of sympathy, a man devoted to the care of sheep. . . . He goes without hesitating to hunt for lost sheep because he has committed himself to the care of the whole hundred, because he understands his work as the fulfilment of his whole trust, because he loves the sheep, and because he knows or imagines what it is to be lost. He does what he does on behalf of the whole flock because he wants to preserve himself as a whole shepherd.[10]

Berry drives us to read this parable economically not because he lacks theological training but because he recognizes how often the church ignores or fails to see the economic import of the biblical witness. How can so many preachers preach on this text but neither call their congregations to the costly caretaking this parable models nor ask them to notice the extent to

9. Berry, *Citizenship Papers*, 93.
10. Berry, *Citizenship Papers*, 93.

which the economy in which they daily live is at odds with the parable's vision? How can scriptural books so concerned with land and the care of it have produced a people of the book with so little concern for the land and economy in which they live?

The other two parables share this pattern of surprising decisions that indicate an economy quite different from that of worldly success. The workers in the vineyard (Matt 20:1–16) is a parable of reversal; Matthew glosses it with the words "The last will be first, and the first will be last" (20:16). Again, though, the reversal is not simply surprising; it is scandalous. And it is scandalous because it challenges us in the place we are most comfortable living—the part of ourselves that wants to be in charge and keep things in order, the part Berry calls the Rational Mind. The Rational Mind cannot imagine a scenario in which a landowner pays more than he is obliged to pay. One pays the least one can, and the laborers are recompensed in strict accordance with their labor. This is the theology of glory applied as an economic principle: one's visible successes are a sign of otherwise invisible superiority. The landowner in the parable, by contrast, cares about the workers and is pleased to be generous. This approach obviously has "spiritual" applications, but again the agrarian reader will insist that the divine economy bears not simply on human salvation but upon human economy as well. This parable challenges close readers to recognize their complicity in an economy at odds with God's economy.

Finally, the sower and the seed reiterates this observed pattern of surprise and scandal within a parable of (often underappreciated) economic scope. It is admittedly an enigmatical parable, one in which the seed is identified by Jesus as the word that is sown (Mark 4:14) but then also becomes different types of reception of the word or even different types of people who hear the word. What is more, in the earliest account of the story—in Mark 4—Jesus indicates that the purpose of this parable and of all parables is a kind of obfuscation: "for those outside, everything comes in parables; in order that 'they may indeed look, but not perceive, and may indeed listen, but not perceive'" (4:11–12).

Nevertheless, the parable functions as a good litmus test for distinguishing a theology of glory and a theology of the cross. The theology of glory, being triumphalist, focuses on the overwhelming crop at the end of the story: "they hear the word and accept it and bear fruit, thirty and sixty and a hundredfold" (4:20). The theologian of the cross—the mad farmer—focuses on the absurd farming practice of the sower. He seems to begin dropping seed as soon as he clears the barn—first on the path, then among rocky ground no good for farming, then among the thorns and weeds that border the field of good soil. It does not require a farmer or even a gardener to confirm for us what common sense asserts: seeds should be planted in the good soil only.

The sower, however, has a larger vision, the same vision that the generous landowner and the shepherd of the lost sheep have. It is an economic vision, but it is not merely a financial one: it is the economy of the Kingdom of God. In this Great Economy it rains on the just and the unjust alike, flowers bloom that no human eye will see, and God is generous beyond all telling. The parable challenges those who follow Jesus and those who proclaim Jesus and his gospel to be willing to be extravagant and even foolish, to engage in scandalous generosity because of the promise that the growth is in God's hands. Again the questions come before us: what would congregations look like if they understood such divine foolishness as central to their mission? And what kind of preaching would insist that economic issues are central to the response of the church to the gospel?

A VISION OF AGRARIANISM IN SCRIPTURE—SUMMARY

The Old and New Testaments are clearly not saying precisely the same things about land, covenant, and agrarianism. However, uniformity is at best a misleading and at worst a dangerous interpretive principle. Far better to note first that both testaments have a central place for issues of land and land economy. They are profoundly aware that creation is a gift and that human beings have a particular role to play in care of the creation. Their faithfulness to God and to the land is good not only for themselves but for the land too. What is more, such fidelity is not abstract or symbolic; on the contrary it is economic and practical. Mistreatment of land and neighbor routinely go hand in hand, and God judges both. Finally, even when emphases vary, we do not find the Old and New Testament at odds with each other. This is not to say that the content of the New Testament follows inevitably from that of the Old, but rather to say that the agrarianism of the Gospels—the parables, mighty deeds, teachings, and metaphors so important to the life of Jesus—springs from the soil of Old Testament agrarianism with its focus on land, economy, and fidelity to the Lord.

Having summarized Berry's central concerns, addressed a theological framework for agrarianism, and provided a scriptural warrant for exploring

Berry's agrarianism further, we turn now to a more innovative question: does agrarianism provide a pattern that is useful to the church; can there be such a thing as an agrarian ecclesiology?

4

An Agrarian Ecclesiology

AGRARIANISM AS A MODEL

IMPERATIVE TO REACHING AN agrarian homiletic is an initial definition, or at least delineation, of the term "agrarian ecclesiology." At its simplest, an agrarian ecclesiology is the application of Berry's insights and claims about the small farm, the farming community, and an agrarian economy to a Christian congregation or community. Some of these applications are direct, such as the belief that a small community—whether farm or congregation—is better situated than a large one to place the proper focus on care (care of place, care of each other, etc.). Some applications are less direct or are even metaphorical, such as the claim that the cycle of the church year is like the cycle of the seasons and that a preacher, like a farmer, aims at a fecundity that is distinct from numerical success.

An agrarian ecclesiology then is not principally a series of claims; it is certainly not advice. It aims at something greater than the imperative. And yet, it must be acknowledged—indeed, insisted upon—that such an ecclesiology is hesitant to claim too great a comprehensiveness. While it strives for fidelity to the lived experiences of congregations and churches, it is not an effort to create a systematic theology of church along agrarian lines. It is probably better to say that it is a vision of church, an act of seeing and describing. Ellen Davis makes a similar point in her delineation of the capaciousness of the agrarian approach to reading Scripture:

> If agrarianism were a technique of literary criticism, even a her-
> meneutic, [we] might more quickly become adept. But it is a
> mind-set, a whole set of understandings, commitments, and prac-
> tices that focus on the most basic of all cultural acts—eating—and
> ramify into virtually every other aspect of public and private life.[1]

To look at a congregation the way Berry looks at a farm is to strive to see it
as fully as possible, at the same time incorporating ignorance and therefore
humility into the very act of apprehension and description. Such an effort
strives to see a congregation's past as well as its present, to see it relative
to the community around it, to see it in the relationships of the people to
God and to each other, and to see it as something not only greater than but
qualitatively different from the sum of its parts.

Perhaps one other way to move towards what the phrase "agrarian
ecclesiology" means is to identify it as a model. A model, as Avery Dulles
makes clear in his groundbreaking *Models of the Church*, aims to be something more than merely an aspect or perspective:

> In selecting the term 'models' rather than 'aspects' or 'dimensions,'
> I wish to indicate my conviction that the Church, like other theo-
> logical realities, is a mystery. Mysteries are realities of which we
> cannot speak directly. If we wish to talk about them at all we must
> draw analogies afforded by our experience of the world.[2]

This understanding jibes incredibly well with Berry's conviction that we
are living within a creation that is holy and ultimately mysterious. In the
end we must acknowledge that all our speaking about God and the gifts of
God—gifts like the church—are inadequate to the task.

If there is in the idea of models a pointing towards the mysterious,
Dulles also wants us to know that there is a modesty in the term as well:
"The peculiarity of models, as contrasted with aspects, is that we cannot
integrate them into a single synthetic vision on the level of articulate,
categorical thought . . . By a kind of mental juggling act, we have to keep
several models in the air at once."[3] Here, too, we see how agrarianism functions well as an ecclesial model. It is not intended to be exclusive, and it is
eager to avoid "a single synthetic vision on the level of articulate, categorical

---

1. Davis, *Scripture, Culture, and Agriculture*, 22.
2. Dulles, *Models of the Church*, 9.
3. Dulles, *Models of the Church*, 10.

thought." It is therefore well-placed to learn from, teach, and interact with other ecclesial models.

Once we begin to make the effort to analyze an agrarian vision or model, we recognize that the single most distinctive element of it is the prominence it gives to the economy and to economic questions. Dulles's book is instructive by way of contrast: none of the five central ecclesial models he proposes is—in his delineation of them anyway—concerned with economics.[4] One might deduce economic principles from them, but their emphases are elsewhere. For Berry, though, all fruitful conversations are rooted finally in what he calls the Great Economy: "The Great Economy, like the Tao or the Kingdom of God, is both known and unknown, visible and invisible, comprehensive and mysterious. It is, thus, the ultimate condition of our experience and of the practical questions rising from our experience."[5]

Knowing, as Berry certainly does, that the word economy comes from the Greek *oikonomia*, meaning "house rules" or "house management," we might say that the Great Economy is the creation understood as God's "house" existing both through and within God's management of it. All that was, is, or will be exists within God's Great Economy. Human economies are perforce subordinate to this Great Economy and are more or less adequate efforts to live within the divine pattern. An agrarian ecclesiology, then, makes central to its attention the relationship between the divine economy and human economies as it plays out in communities of faith.

At the heart of agrarian disappointment with and anger at contemporary human economies is their fallacious claim to be comprehensive and to serve as ultimate arbiters. If the Great Economy is our measure, then economics *qua* economics ought to acknowledge limits and boundaries; in actual practice, Berry contends, it rarely does:

> it is astonishing, and of course discouraging, to see economics
> now elevated to the position of ultimate justifier and explainer of
> all the affairs of our daily life, and competition enshrined as the
> sovereign principle and ideal of economics.[6]

---

4. While it is difficult to prove a negative, the Index for Dulles's book is instructive: the word "economy" appears only once, in a passing reference to the title of a letter by American Roman Catholic bishops, *Economic Justice for All*.

5. Berry, *Home Economics*, 56–57.

6. Berry, *What Are People For?*, 129.

It can be hard to quantify Berry's claim that the economy is now the "ultimate justifier and explainer of all the affairs of our daily life," but pastors who have preached an Advent or Ash Wednesday sermon know in their bones that Berry is right. What more ridiculous effort is there than preachers standing up in early December and urging their people to "Watch" and "Wait" in the midst of the economic orgy of impatience that is the "holiday season"? A similar feeling of impotence often comes to church leaders who propose paying more for church supplies and services by purchasing them locally and bypassing chain stores and online giants. The plain truth is that the contemporary church routinely serves the economy in ways that are indistinguishable from the stores, companies, and municipal organizations around them.

A competitive economy like ours that understands itself as limitless is, by this very understanding, willing to be destructive in limitless ways. If a company can charge less by bringing products in from a great distance, then competition demands that it does so, and ecological questions like fuel consumption, air quality, and the like cannot be factored in. Certainly questions cannot be asked about how the product is mined or built or assembled at the other end, nor how the people are treated who mine or build or assemble. As Berry puts it, "The danger of the ideal of competition is that it neither proposes nor implies any limits. It proposes simply to lower costs at any cost. . . . It does not hesitate at the destruction of the life of a family or the life of a community."[7]

An agrarian ecclesiology, then, challenges such inadequate understandings of the economy and encourages us to ask our practical economic questions in the light of the Great Economy. Here are a few such challenging questions. How would a congregation's relationship to its community change if it committed itself to the local economy? How would a congregation's self-awareness change if it saw ecological issues not in competition with economic issues (e.g., "We'd like to line the roof with solar panels, but it costs too much") but rather in partnership with God's greater economy? How would a congregation's witness and evangelism change if it invited people into a prophetic relationship towards the competitive economy of the culture around them?

That the church is by and large not asking these questions seems hard to deny. That Berry perceives the church as a part of the problem rather than a part of the solution is indisputable. When asked what, if anything,

7. Berry, *What Are People For?*, 131.

he hears from preachers that offers hope, Berry replies, "Not much, because to me the economic question is paramount. I think the Old Order Amish have survived as a community, moreover a Christian community, because they have understood Luke 10:25–37 [the parable of the good Samaritan] as an economic imperative."[8] And when asked how he would move a church community towards an agrarian model of church, his reply is equally concerned with the economic: "Ask them to consider that they practice their religion largely by their economic life. And then ask them to ask themselves how much they actually know about their economic life. What do they know of the human and ecological costs of the things they buy?"[9] These words elucidate the model of church here proposed, a model wherein economic questions are central because practice follows belief in ways that go far beyond personal piety. Further, Berry's words indicate the extent to which churches are willingly but often unwittingly participating in practices at odds with their stated beliefs about God and all that God has made.

One final point needs to be made in considering the centrality of economics to the agrarian model: while this section reflects the extent to which Berry's writings about culture and economy are cautionary and contrarian, it should be noted that one goal of changing economic practices is an increase in pleasure and even in joy. One of Berry's most constant laments is that, "More and more, our farms and forests resemble our factories and offices, which in turn more and more resemble prisons—why else should we be so eager to escape them?"[10] By way of contrast he continues to offer a vision of work as something that, done well, contains the seed and often the fruit of pleasure within it. He continues to speak for an economy where "our pleasure would not be merely an addition or by-product or reward; it would be both an empowerment of our work and its indispensable measure."[11] This kind of language gets remarkably close to traditional Christian ideas about vocation: work is a response to a calling; it is both useful and fulfilling; in the midst of difficulties, there is nonetheless the possibility of pleasure and satisfaction in the doing of it. Perhaps one of the reasons pastors have to keep reminding their people of this shared vocation

8. Berry, letter to author, November 2019.

9. Berry, letter to the author, November 2019.

10. Berry, *What Matters?*, 99–100.

11. Berry, *What Matters?*, 100.

is that so many people now do work that they do not feel called to, work that is done for the sake of an income only.

Berry is confident that the notion that pleasure can be found in healthy economy is not mere nostalgia on his part, nor is it pie-in-the-sky hopefulness. It is rather a radical claim, one that takes Christians back to their own theological tradition. He quotes approvingly from Revelation: "Thou art worthy, O Lord, to receive glory and honour and power: for thou hast created all things, and for thy pleasure they are and were created" (Rev 4:11).[12] These words, taken seriously, compel Christians to re-examine a merely utilitarian exploitation of "natural resources," and remind us that God's pleasure—and by extension ours—is one measure of our response to the world around us. To take no pleasure in what pleases God is a grievous failure, just as is taking pleasure in actions and beliefs that are displeasing to God. Berry is, as always, clear about where his loyalties lie:

> This bountiful and lovely thought that all creatures are pleasing to God—and potentially pleasing, therefore, to us—is unthinkable from the point of view of an economy divorced from pleasure. . . . Where is our comfort but in the free, uninvolved, finally mysterious beauty and grace of this world that we did not make, that has no price? Where is our sanity but there? Where is our pleasure but in working and resting kindly in the presence of this world?[13]

A key result of the centrality of economics in agrarianism is that an agrarian ecclesiology takes with almost stunning earnestness the gift of place. The place has been here since before we arrived, and it will be here after we are gone. It comes to us as a gift, and it calls forth from us faith and labor. A contrast might make this point clearer. Most people have had the experience of being in a place that is barely a place at all: a mall that looks like a hundred other malls, a fast-food restaurant indistinguishable from the rest in the chain, a corporate office with rows of identical cubicles. How different a church building is, especially when it is home to a vibrant community. It is, quite literally, like nowhere else in the world. Its relationship to its municipality, its architecture and art, its programs and worship: all of these fairly shout to the members of the community that they are receiving the gift of a particular place and time and calling.

One place to begin to see what Berry has to say about the significance of place is his essay "Faustian Economics: Hell Hath No Limits." Here he

12. Berry, *What Matters?*, 98.

13. Berry, *What Matters?*, 99–100.

argues that what ails our culture—and by extension our denominations and congregations—is an enthusiasm for growth and success without limits. Berry makes this assertion early in the essay:

> in keeping with our unrestrained consumptiveness, the commonly accepted basis of our economy is the supposed possibility of limitless growth, limitless wants, limitless wealth, limitless natural resources, limitless energy, and limitless debt. The idea of a limitless economy implies and requires a doctrine of general human limitlessness: *all* are entitled to pursue without limit whatever they conceive as desirable—a license that classifies the most exalted Christian capitalist with the lowliest pornographer.[14]

Berry then turns to Christopher Marlowe's play *The Tragical History of Doctor Faustus*; he sees in this Renaissance text a pertinent reflection on the ills—indeed, the wickedness—of limitlessness. When Faustus asks the devil Mephistophilis, "How comes it then that thou art out of hell?" Mephistophilis replies, "Why, this is hell, nor am I out of it. . . . Hell hath no limits, nor is circumscribed / In one self place, but where we [the damned] are is hell, / And where hell is must we ever be."[15] In other words, for those who reject heaven, hell is everywhere, and thus is limitless. This is a stunning reversal of typical conceptions of hell as a prison. In Marlowe's understanding, lack of place—the fact of being uprooted—is part and parcel of damnation. Place and location are gifts of the creator; to seek to live beyond proper boundaries is to be enticed to a form of life that is finally infernal.

This is a bedrock claim for Berry, one that permeates all he writes and does—place and boundary as central to our creatureliness and to our creaturely health. In his earlier essays, such as "A Native Hill," he tells the autobiographical story of his path back to his home place after a life that looked to be headed out and away. Of his decision to reject the pattern of so many writers—to leave the countryside and dwell in the city or on the campus—and to return to Kentucky, he writes, "My return, which at first had been hesitant and tentative, grew wholehearted and sure . . . And once that was settled I began to *see* the place with a new clarity and a new understanding."[16] In such words we can see him moving towards the insights he makes in "Faustian Economics." He is not making an assertion akin to glib Christian claims that "God is everywhere" such that one can

---

14. Berry, *What Matters?*, 43.
15. Berry, *What Matters?*, 46.
16. Berry, *Recollected Essays 1965–1980*, 79.

worship God anywhere. There is a philosophical sense in which such claims are abstractly defensible, but they cannot be lived by actual creatures. We cannot worship God anywhere but only in the place we actually are; we may trust that God is everywhere, but that is a claim that only has value when we get specific. Human beings are embodied creatures who need to be located to be fully human. For the damned souls in Marlowe's play, lack of place—we might say lack of home—is not an amelioration to their pains but is at the very heart of it. Wherever they go, they carry their homelessness with them.

From this gift of place come several consequent claims. Principal among these is the preference for what can be accomplished locally and in relationship to the land and community near at hand. This preference inevitably entails a further preference for the small over the large: Berry argues that small farms with a rich and complex crop are preferable to large monocrop farms heavily reliant on chemicals and technology to turn a profit, and an agrarian ecclesiology argues equally that small congregations are better suited to the actual work of the church than large ones. They are able to be more flexible and adaptive than a larger community; such flexibility makes it easier for them to think of themselves as local communities responsive to local needs. None of this implies that smaller congregations must or will think of themselves in these ways, only that smaller congregations will find themselves with fewer obstacles to agrarianism as practiced in a church setting.

One way to get a handle on this preference for the local is to recognize that for Berry agrarianism "is primarily a practice, a set of attitudes, a loyalty, and a passion" and again that agrarianism "is a culture at the same time that it is an economy."[17] Therefore, the "agrarian mind is . . . not regional or national, let alone global, but local."[18] What this means for the life of the church right now is that virtually all urban and suburban—as well as many rural—congregations are not in fact agrarian in their outlook. Like the rest of the culture, they live far from the things of the land literally and figuratively. Thus a rural congregation that "produces" food for a food bank by buying it from the large-scale grocery store which brings in food from hundreds or thousands of miles away is no more agrarian than a suburban congregation supplying a food bank in just the same way. A congregation that dreams of bringing in new members by the use of extensive technology

17. Berry, *Citizenship Papers*, 115.
18. Berry, *Citizenship Papers*, 116.

for distance worship is not agrarian in its outlook regardless of where the church building is located.

Juxtaposed to the agrarian mind for Berry is the system called industrialism, and this distinction also helps clarify the agrarian preference for the local. For it is the nature of industrialism to be something quite different from agrarianism: where agrarianism strives to be an economy working in tandem with a culture, industrialism aims to be an economy working in every culture and in disregard of any culture. It aspires to as a goal that which is for Mephistophilis and for the damned a curse—to be without limits. Its goal is to create a market for purchasable goods that cannot be created locally, and then to produce those goods at a price that is only apparently inexpensive. The true expense in mining, fuel, transport, and the like is hidden from the consumer's eyes, though of course it is not hidden from the planet—from the creation—itself. As Berry writes, "Like the rich man of the parable, the industrialist thinks to escape the persistent obligations of the human condition by means of 'much goods laid up for many years'—by means, in other words, of quantities: resources, supplies, stockpiles, funds, reserves. But this is a grossly oversimplifying dream and, thus, a dangerous one."[19]

All of this means for a congregation that seeking to embrace and enact an agrarian ecclesiology is a complicated act of rebellion. On the one hand no congregation can cut itself off entirely from the current cultural addiction to rampant industrialism: there is a basic need to heat and light the building, and it is no simple or inexpensive matter to find alternatives to gas and electricity tied to the oil and coal industries. There is a need for telephones, for office paper, and for a dozen other objects and technologies tied to industrialism. Just as an individual, short of an apprenticeship among the Amish, cannot embrace agrarianism in one fell swoop, so too with a congregation. However, even beginning to think with a bias towards the agrarian and the local, and with a bias against the industrial and the multi-national, can be remarkably freeing. What if congregations were intentional about their relationships to local farms and farmer markets? Or if they made the commitment to buy materials and services locally? What if they committed over time to reduce or eliminate on-line buying? What if congregations with declining numbers saw this as an opportunity to abandon large sanctuaries for smaller rooms, not simply as an act of good liturgy but as an extended effort to reduce the use of expensive oil and

19. Berry, *Citizenship Papers*, 229.

electricity? These steps are agrarian responses to an industrial society, and they have about them a kind of basic sanity.

Another gift of the emphasis on place is that the people in the community are encouraged to see their marginality not as a blight but as a benefit. Such a change would be an extraordinary lifting of burdens for a great many congregations. Over the last sixty years mainline denominations have found themselves increasingly sidelined by the industrial and technological world in which we increasingly live. Understanding this shift as a gift and not only a burden is the theology of the cross working itself out in the church: small and marginal congregations are given the gift of seeing the scandal of the gospel manifest in their shared life. For them the foolishness of the cross expressed in a countercultural community life is visible to their eyes and not simply to their imagination.

Similarly, the gift of place means that a proper concern for form is encouraged. That which strives to be large and successful can rarely afford to ask questions about proper limits and boundaries: it is hard to imagine prosperous congregations—or those whose goal is to be prosperous—making hard decisions that might affect attendance or giving numbers. A small congregation, however, can ask and address questions differently.

Another major aspect of an agrarian ecclesiology has already been implied—a general mistrust or even distrust of the patterns of thought and speech and action associated with empire. Already addressed has been concern about striving for greater size and cultural influence. We can add to this a similar concern that what claims to be missional is often simply part and parcel of the larger culture—growth, product, market share, and the like repackaged in Christian wrapping. An agrarian ecclesiology not only challenges the notion that the church needs to be more like the culture around it; it challenges the notion that the tools of empire are neutral and can be easily borrowed and adapted for use by the church.

In particular an agrarian ecclesiology looks askance at the so-called gift of greater and greater technology. Nothing is more American than the claim that a new machine or gadget or device will reduce work and increase productivity. Little has been more tempting to the church of the last hundred years than the corporate model and its love of technology. Congregations apply a business model to their structure, and technology becomes central to how the church expresses and communicates its self-understanding. The point here is not nostalgic; rather, the point is to draw a congregation into a conversation about the real and full price of what they are doing. What prices must be paid—by the earth, by the congregation, by the relationships among members—when a congregation is increasingly dependent on technology to worship and to communicate?

Undergirding all that has come so far is Berry's doctrine of creation. He has repeatedly made it clear that "I take literally the statement in the Gospel of John that God loves the world."[20] Indeed, one of Berry's chief complaints against the church is that it does not take seriously the love of God's creation that it professes:

> The holiness of life is obscured by modern Christianity also by the idea that the only holy place is the built church. . . . It is understandably difficult for modern Americans to think of their dwellings and workplaces as holy, because most of these are, in fact, places of desecration.[21]

In other words, through their buildings Christians engage in a functional dualism. Though they profess to love creation, they see their church buildings as the locus of God's attention and approval; as a result, they do not see their homes and workplaces—let alone the pastures and the fields—as sacred. This divorce between so-called religious places and so-called secular places is indicative of a larger chasm in Christian practice. Berry is troubled by "a dualism that manifests itself in several ways: as a cleavage, a radical discontinuity, between Creator and creature, spirit and matter, religion and nature, religion and economy, worship and work, and so on. This dualism, I think, is the most destructive disease that afflicts us."[22] An agrarian model for church accepts none of these bifurcations. It is troubled both by those who believe that the earth is a mere resource given by God for our use and by those who have a concern for ecology but do not see that they are themselves a part of the problem.

Yet another aspect of an agrarian ecclesiology is a concern for membership—that is, for a fuller understanding of what belonging means. Agrarianism is inevitably about interrelationship: it bespeaks belonging; it places an emphasis on care. The fundamental claim of a community touched by these insights is that the community belongs to God and to one another. One of the fundamental acts of such a community, then, is reminding people of the God who calls them into relationship, of re-membering them through word and water, bread and wine, fellowship and service.

20. Berry, *Another Turn of the Crank*, 89.
21. Berry, *Sex, Economy, Freedom and Community*, 100.
22. Berry, *Sex, Economy, Freedom and Community*, 105.

Berry uses the word "membership" repeatedly in his Port William fiction as a description of the relationships between people of the same generation and of people across generations. D. Brent Laytham has presented a compelling argument that what Berry means by membership is largely what the church means by the *communio sanctorum*. While a rehearsal of his entire argument is beyond the scope of this book, it is worth taking a moment to focus on Laytham's key point—that much of the church in the twenty-first century lives in such separation from the land and the creation that they are functionally gnostic. He complains justly of the "all too common tendency among Christians: they think and feel that they are homeless, or they believe in a heaven that competes with—and calls them away from—this earth."[23]

Laytham goes on to distinguish Berry's understanding of membership from such a perspective: "Unlike a Gnosticized *communio sanctorum*, Berry's membership is placed. It is the membership of Port William, not the membership of anywhere or of nowhere. The common ground the members share is the very foundation on which membership rests."[24] Literally dozens of passages from the fiction—and from the poetry and essays, as well—could be cited in explication of Berry's fundamentally religious understanding of membership, but two will suffice to elucidate what is at stake for Berry in this term. In one of his most autobiographical novels, *A World Lost*, the narrator Andy Catlett reflects in the final paragraph of the book: "slowly I have learned that my true home is not just this place but is also the company of immortals with whom I have lived here day by day."[25] This is a rich, multi-dimensional understanding of location and of being located. It is a perspective that is theologically coherent, and yet it is a perspective largely absent in practice in far too many Christian communities today. In suburban congregations where most members drive to worship and think of church primarily as a building, the most common relationship with those in other pews is often nothing more than knowing a name; and the relationship to those who have gone before is largely ignorance.

How different such ignorance is from the sense of membership expressed by one of Berry's most fully realized characters, Burley Coulter. Burley is hardly a model figure. He would rather hunt than go to church, and in many of the stories in which he features, his sexual adventures and

---

23. Laytham, "'Membership Includes the Dead,'" 174.

24. Laytham, "'Membership Includes the Dead,'" 175.

25. Berry, *World Lost*, 151.

his fondness for alcohol figure prominently. And yet Berry clearly admires Burley, seeing in him someone who can speak for the membership from its margin. Towards the end of the short story "The Wild Birds," Burley builds on Andy Catlett's understanding that a community is bound to each other in both space and time:

> I'm saying that the ones who have been here have been the way they were, and the ones of us who are here now are the way we are and to *know* that is the only chance we've got, dead and living, to be here together. . . . The way we are, we are members of each other. All of us. Everything. The difference ain't who is a member and who is not, but in who knows it and who don't.[26]

Like Andy Catlett, Burley sees the membership extending across time. Beyond that, he also sees that membership acknowledges shortcoming and limitation across time—acknowledges them and forgives them and enfolds them into the history and embrace of the community. Even more, he expresses eloquently what many in the church fail to understand—that the greatest difference among people in the membership or the *communio sanctorum* is not between insiders and outsiders, but rather between those who recognize that all are a part of it and those who do not. A pastor who preached a congregation into recognizing that they are a community formed by God, connected to those who came before and those who will come after, would have done a good day's work!

AGRARIAN ESCHATOLOGY

One final topic must be addressed within an agrarian model of church—eschatology. It is tempting to avoid it because eschatology is an immense field unto itself, and it is also an area of Christian thought where approaches and interpretations vary widely. And yet, Berry's understanding of creation and of membership implies and even requires some wrestling with questions of ultimate purpose and meaning. Further, the agrarian understanding of church, concerned as it is with membership and creation, is incomplete without a vision of fulfillment. While Berry does not offer anything like a fully visualized apocalyptic model, he clearly does believe that the meaning that inheres in creation and in creatures requires a prophetic and even visionary understanding of time and place.

26. Berry, *Wild Birds*, 136–37.

Unlike Berry, many Christians fall into one of two extremes. Some are fiercely literal about the end times, weaving a complex timetable out of Daniel, the words of Jesus, Revelation, and other apocalyptic passages. There are literary problems to this approach, of course, but there is also the perennial problem of dualism: just as many have a dislocated relationship to creation, so too eschatologists of this type have a dislocated understanding of eschatology. To the extent that it means anything at all, eschatology in this view is not about the marriage of heaven and earth but about their long-anticipated divorce. It is largely a question of chronology and sorting out winners and losers: when will Jesus return, what will his final victory be like, who will go and who will be left behind? Such an approach might charitably be described as naïve literalism, but it would be more accurate to see it as the inevitable concomitant of a truncated understanding of what Revelation means by "a new heaven and a new earth" (Rev 21:1).

At the other end of the spectrum are Christians who believe themselves too liberal or modern to take apocalyptic passages very seriously, let alone literally. This approach looks as though it might align itself more closely with Berry's agrarianism and with a love of the creation as God has made. However, this approach, too, is a form of dualism, dividing past from present and biblical promises from contemporary hopes. It evinces a chronological snobbery—a belief that biblical writers are unable to distinguish the literal from the poetic; it therefore possesses an unwarranted confidence that our so-called progress has taken us beyond these ancient concerns.

Scripture is more nuanced and also more tactile than either of these extremes. It is anything but dualistic, speaking of the last things in words that point to physical and material realities—cities, trees, lions and lambs, etc.—but always in terms that beg to be recognized as imagery, metaphor, and symbolism. This is perforce indirect discourse, and yet it is clear that the biblical witness is to a resurrection of the body and a renewal of the creation that incorporates both the spiritual and the material. Despite the views of some Christians, Scripture bears witness that earth will not vanish or find itself translated into spirit; neither will the spirit leave the body behind and go to someplace called heaven. On the contrary, "I saw a new heaven and a new earth; for the first heaven and the first earth had passed away. . . . And I saw the holy city, the new Jerusalem, coming down out of heaven. . . . And I heard a loud voice from the throne saying, 'See, the home of God is among mortals'" (Rev 21:1–3). This is a vision of the last things that finds resonance in the writings of Berry and that requires would-be agrarian theologians to take eschatology seriously.

At the center of an agrarian eschatology is a recognition of the goodness of the creation and the interconnectedness of such things as spirit and matter. Berry's understanding of this interconnectedness infuses all of his writing. Often it remains implicit or exists in narrative as an atmosphere or an unspoken assumption among the membership. Sometimes, however, it is front and center, as in this brief poem:

> If there are a "chosen few"
> then I am not one of them,
> if an "elect," well then
> I have not been elected.
> I am one who is knocking
> at the door. I am one whose foot
> is on the bottom rung.
> But I know that Heaven's
> bottom rung is Heaven
> though the ladder is standing
> on the earth where I work
> by day and at night sleep
> with my head upon a stone.[27]

What is worth noting first is what is rejected—the language of those who favor a literalist understanding of heaven and of the end times. Berry wants no truck with the dualistic and often presumptuous language of "chosen few" or the "elect."[28] Instead he positions himself through an allusion to

---

27. Berry, *This Day*, 283.

28. It is not possible in a footnote to address fully the extent to which Berry's words in this poem and in other passages put him in tension with or even opposition to biblical ideas of election and of a chosen people. However, two observations seem helpful. First, Berry's love for the creation—all of the creation—pushes him in the direction of universalism. In response to a letter in which I asked Berry which verses of Scripture continue to be meaningful to him over time, he emphasizes those that speak of God's spirit present in all living things. Among others that are similar, he cites Ps 104:28–30 ("when you give it to them, they gather it up; / when you open your hand, they are filled with good things. / When you hide your face, they are dismayed; / when you take away their breath, they die / and return to their dust. / When you send forth your spirit, they are created; / and you renew the face of the ground.") and Luke 10:25–37, the parable of the good Samaritan. Such a response certainly indicates that Berry prefers a capacious reading of God's providence to a narrow reading of God's election. Second, though I cannot prove my reading of this poem, it seems evident to me that Berry's quarrel with terms like "chosen few" and "elect" is aimed less at the biblical witness than at American

the words of Jesus: "Knock and the door will be opened to you" (Matt 7:7). Then he draws in the quintessential biblical witness to the interconnection of heaven and earth: Jacob and his dream or vision of a ladder. Like Jacob, Berry recognizes himself as of earth, one who sleeps "with my head upon a stone." And yet, he also knows that "Heaven's / bottom rung is Heaven / though the ladder is standing / on the earth." The creation is seamless; earth participates in heaven and is not obliterated or rendered meaningless by it.

Perhaps this interconnection is seen most clearly in Berry's fiction. In novel after novel, in story after story, his most sympathetic characters are people of the land—farming families, hired hands, lawyers who work in defense of farming, and the like. By contrast, his most unsympathetic characters are figures who disconnect themselves from the land—farmers who create large monoculture farms so they can work from an office and people who crave the city and who think themselves too good for manual labor. One of Berry's most sympathetic characters is the farmer Jack Beechum, Old Jack. Because Jack is the central character of a full-length novel, we see through him a large number of agrarian themes: aversion to the progress promised by technology, love for the land and the people of the land, preference for the local and the small over the distant and the large.

In one of the central scenes of *The Memory of Old Jack*, Jack has recovered from fifteen years of financial woes largely of his own making and finds himself with nothing more to show for it than the farm with which he started out. He returns to his farm with his debt finally paid and the mortgage from the bank in his shirt pocket. Berry might have made this a moment about success or second chances, but he does not. Instead he offers a moment saturated with meaning and as full of heaven as of earth:

> . . . he comes in sight of the upland fields of his own place: the house and outbuildings and barns, the winter-deadened sod of the pastures, the veil of green wheat over last year's crop lands. . . . And now it seems to him that his soul breaks open, like a dull coal, shattering brilliance around him. He has been gone but little more than two hours, and yet he returns as from a long voyage or a war. Now he does consciously feel the open sky above him, the eye of heaven clear upon him.[29]

This is visionary language: Jack sees the old world with new eyes; he is reborn, transformed by his return to a place he has not known until now.

---

evangelicals whose understanding and use of these terms trouble him.

29. Berry, *Memory of Old Jack*, 122.

Much as in the poem where "Heaven's / bottom rung is Heaven / though the ladder is standing / on the earth," so Jack knows earth better because "the eye of heaven [is] clear upon him." What's more, his vision of heaven is clarified by his renewed vision of earth.

That Berry wants us to see Jack's transformation as religious in the best sense becomes explicit in the following paragraph. Jack reflects on the experience that he is having as he looks upon his farm:

> Words come to him: "Yea, though I walk through the valley of the shadow of death. . . . Yea, though I walk through the valley of the shadow of death, I will fear no evil"—the words of the old psalm that Nancy had made him repeat when he was a boy until he would remember it all his life. He had always been able to see through those words to what they were about. He could see the green pastures and the still waters and the shepherd bringing the sheep down out of the hills in the evening to drink. It comes to him that he never understood them before, but that he does now. The man who first spoke the psalm . . . knew that his origin was in nothing that he or any man had done, and that he could do nothing sufficient to his needs. And he looked finally beyond those limits and saw the world still there, potent and abounding. . . . [Jack] saw that he would be distinguished not by what he was or anything he might become but by what he served. Beyond him was the peace and rest and joy that he desired."[30]

To attempt to draw out from this luminous passage the various threads of agrarian thought would be a kind of futile vivisection: the threads weave a tapestry suffused with Berry's and Jack's vision of the meaning of the land and of life itself. Nevertheless, a few themes are worthy of note. First, the use of the twenty-third Psalm invokes a key scriptural touchpoint and does it in such a way that the shepherd of the poem is both the LORD and also the shepherd who wrote the psalm. In other words, the psalm is not simply a metaphor about God but is, in Jack's understanding, an understanding of God and creation that comes out of the lived experience of a shepherd, an actual agrarian. What is more, Jack now has what we might inadequately call a theological understanding of the psalm—how we are cared for by a Being who knows our boundaries and our needs and loves us precisely as boundaried, needy creatures. And beyond that, Jack realizes that we are called to serve what is beyond us and what will outlast us: "Beyond him was the peace and rest and joy that he desired."

30. Berry, *Memory of Old Jack*, 122–23.

Jack provides us one of the clearest visions of heaven and earth and of their intertwining—but certainly not the only one. Indeed, one other figure and one other extended passage are necessary for this brief overview of an agrarian eschatology. Jayber Crow is the figure, and the passage comes from the novel of the same name. It is an even more explicitly visionary passage than that of Jack Beechum, and it shows how central people and community (and not just land) are to Berry's eschatology. Jayber is the local barber of Port William, and he is also the custodian at the local church:

> One day when I went up [to the church] to work, sleepiness overcame me and I lay down on the floor behind the back pew to take a nap. Waking or sleeping (I couldn't tell which), I saw all the people gathered there who had ever been there. I saw them as I had seen them from the back pew, where I sat with Uncle Othy (who would not come in any further) while Aunt Cordie sang in the choir, and I saw them as I had seen them (from the back pew) on the Sunday before. I saw them in all the times past and to come, all somehow there in their own time and in all time and in no time: the cheerfully working and singing women, the men quiet or reluctant or shy, the weary, the troubled in spirit, the sick, the lame, the desperate, the dying, the little children tucked into the pews beside their elders, the young married couples full of visions, the old men with their dreams, the parents proud of their children, the grandparents with tears in their eyes, the pairs of young lovers attentive only to each other on the edge of the world, the grieving widows and widowers, the mothers and fathers of children newly dead, the proud, the humble, the attentive, the distracted—I saw them all. I saw the creases crisscrossed on the backs of the men's necks, their work-thickened hands, the Sunday dresses faded with washing. They were just there. They said nothing, and I said nothing. I seemed to love them all with a love that was mine merely because it included me. When I came to myself again, my face was wet with tears.[31]

Jayber's description is full of tropes typical of apocalyptic or eschatological visions—be they biblical or from the pen of Dante, Milton, and others. He does not know if he is awake or asleep. He is both in time and beyond time. He is both an observer and a participant. He sees people in different times and modes simultaneously, and he sees them both as individuals and as examples or types of people. Further, meaning is inherent in the vision; that is, unlike less visionary passages, the scene requires of

31. Berry, *Jayber Crow,* 164–65.

the reader an understanding that what Jayber sees is true in ways that are perhaps ineffable but are not open to doubt or question. A hypothetical reader who replied, "Well, maybe he was only dreaming and none of this really matters" has profoundly misunderstood the passage.

It is always risky mining the ineffable for nuggets of truth, but the claim that this passage is visionary and even eschatological in an agrarian mode requires explication. Three insights seem especially relevant. First, the agrarian eschatology at work here suggests that linear time as most people experience it is not a sufficient lens for seeing meaning aright. To know the love that creates and sustains the world, one must see people "in all the times past and to come, all somehow there in their own time and in all time and in no time." This should hardly be surprising. To take simply the largest example, the eschatology at work in Revelation is notoriously slippery on the issue of time. Scenes that appear to follow chronologically actually loop back and reiterate or reenvisage events from earlier in the text; passages appearing to foretell the future look backwards and are laced through and through with Old Testament references; much that seems to concern linear or horizontal time turns out in fact to be vertical and refer to the way in which earthly events are mirrored or explicated in heaven.

Second, an agrarian eschatology is particular and perspicacious, seeing people with emotional attentiveness and in the light of grace. The people in this passage are as particular as the narrator's aunt and uncle; they are the young and old, the sick and well; they are recognizable by the creases on their neck and the Sunday dresses "faded from washing." And, within that attentiveness, they are also seen as something larger than themselves alone, not as types but as creaturely participants in the larger creation—"the young married couples full of visions" and "the old men with the dreams" all taking part in a community that stretches as far back as ancient Israel: "I will pour out my spirit on all flesh; your sons and your daughter shall prophesy, your old men shall dream dreams, and your young men shall see visions" (Joel 2:28).

Third, Jayber's vision is a profoundly subjective experience. That is, it is local in the fullest sense: its vision points beyond itself not by denying its place or its localized vocabulary, but by embracing them. Just as Revelation is inextricably a vision produced in the Roman Empire of the first century of the Common Era, the *Divine Comedy* in medieval Italy, and *Paradise Lost* in seventeenth-century England, so Jayber sees that-which-is-beyond as an illumination of that-which-is. He is also a participant in the vision.

The light of love that suffuses the scene includes him: "I seemed to love them all with a love that was mine merely because it included me. When I came to myself again, my face was wet with tears."

On the one hand, it is risky to construct an agrarian eschatology in response to a poem and passages from two novels. On the other hand, perhaps poetry and narrative are precisely the modes by which an eschatology is best expressed. Certainly Daniel and Mark 13 and Revelation point in that direction. Through such genres it is possible to speak beyond the literal, to speak of the marriage of heaven and earth without falling into a functional dualism. Berry does not offer us a timeline or a roadmap for the apocalypse, but he does offer pictures and images that convey meaning. The eschatology he offers the church is neither a literalist coda nor a modernist form of pretending; it is, rather, baked into the creation—the Great Economy—itself. Heaven and earth, body and soul, past and present and future, people of all types and places: though we often see them now as discrete from each other, the vision of a final consummation does not lie. What is now broken and incomplete will one day be healed and complete. God will re-member all that has been divided.

5

An Agrarian Homiletic

Preceding chapters have established several key claims. First, agrarianism—especially the agrarianism of Wendell Berry—offers a perspective and a set of resources which the contemporary American church genuinely needs. Second, this agrarianism is not incidental but fundamental to Scripture. In the Hebrew Scriptures God, people, and land constitute the central elements of covenant; the three are a kind of braid that could not exist if any one of them were missing. The relationship of the New Testament to land is perhaps more complex; in the parables, teachings, and mighty deeds of Jesus, we see how New Testament authors take Old Testament ideas about land as a kind of *cantus firmus* which opens into new polyphony when interacting with the coming of Christ. Or, to stay with musical metaphors, land and covenant are a leitmotif that runs through the Gospels. Third, Berry's agrarianism shares ideas and commitments with Luther's theology of the cross. Fourth, agrarianism's complex web of relationships with the needs of the church, with Scripture, and with theology means that it is possible to construct an agrarian ecclesiology. This ecclesiology places particular emphasis on economy, place, membership, limitation and ignorance, rejection of industrialism and triumphalism, distrust of technophilia, a non-dualistic doctrine of creation, and eschatology.

An agrarian homiletic incorporates these various claims and commitments, and it is also something more than simply a restatement of certain biblical and theological claims. It is rather a creative application of those claims to the task of preaching. Much as land and land management are a part of the scriptural story, much as Luther's theology of the cross tells an alternative narrative to the theology of glory, so agrarian preachers need to imagine themselves and their community as part of the larger story, as connected to a set of relationships that are beyond their sight and that are not principally of their own making.

A part of the reason that imagination is so central is that agrarian preaching is not a kind of preaching aimed only or even principally at rural congregations or at congregations in farming regions. It is rather the interpretation of an agrarian ecclesiology within the broad range of situations in which preachers find themselves. Urban and suburban congregations ought to be able to reflect an agrarian ecclesiology and homiletic that is fitting to their own situation.

Further, because of the need for imagination, an agrarian homiletic is by its nature flexible and responsive to context, varying from place to place and from preacher to preacher; such local adaptation is part and parcel of the agrarian approach. It avoids advice but is more than willing to express enthusiasm for some matters and skepticism for others. It might be most helpful to say that an agrarian homiletic would be recognizable as a set of related commitments and preferences. To frame this chapter in the form of a question, we might ask ourselves this: What are the specific ways that agrarianism, as expressed by Wendell Berry, can help a congregation or community to reimagine itself, and how does a preacher proclaim the gospel in ways that both reflect and encourage this new agrarian self-understanding?

Wendell Berry has a fondness for enumerated lists, for creating a chain of interrelated claims. Given all that has been written so far, it is probably not hard to see why. Berry understands love, order, and membership to be fundamental truths at all levels of the creation—the cosmic and the local, the natural and also the communal. As such, to move from one claim to another is to enact for his readers on a small scale the patterns that obtain at all scales.[1]

An agrarian homiletic, then, may be expressed as a set of interrelated claims. Such a presentation does not imply that the list is exhaustive. It does imply that this agrarian approach deserves to be seen as a genuine homiletic, i.e., a coherent model for the act of preaching.

---

1. Examples of Berry's fondness for list-making can be found in many places, including the essays "The Pleasures of Eating," "The Future of Agriculture," and "Starting from Loss."

1. Scripture ought to be read through the lens of its own contexts—historical, literary, biographical, and more—so as to achieve a prophetic reading "from below."

2. To read and preach "from below" requires of preachers a theological hermeneutic that is either explicitly drawn from or implicitly akin to Luther's theology of the cross.

3. Agrarian preachers ought to address economic issues through a range of approaches that goes far deeper than the annual stewardship drive; the economic claims of Scripture, the lived economic principles of the congregation, and the congregation's relationship to the local economy are all appropriate loci for preaching.

4. The importance of place for the agrarian preacher means that such a preacher must be a local theologian; further, such a preacher deepens ties within the community by applying agrarian metaphors to congregational membership.

5. Agrarian preaching expands and deepens the congregation's understanding of membership; three central foci in this effort are an attention to the particularities of church history, engagement with the lectionary, and a regular explication of financial stewardship.

6. In response to a culture that is addicted to technology, the agrarian ought to awaken people to the true price of technological change and to the alternative, tactile vision of community offered by the church.

7. The sacraments ought to be preached in such a way that the community sees in them a direct and tangible link to the Great Economy, to the fields and vines and waters of God's creation.

8. Agrarian preaching should be eschatological; it should draw a community's attention not away from time and place but to the ways the Great Economy exists in and through time; it ought to encourage a community to see their particular setting in light of God's larger purposes; and it ought to offer confident hope when confronting the excesses of human economies.

9. Even as agrarianism pays special attention to pattern—the order of creation, the economy of a farm—so an agrarian preacher must consider the pattern of the sermon crucial to the sermon's meaning.

SCRIPTURAL CONTEXT

It is a cliché of contemporary scriptural exegesis and homiletics to say that context matters. Annotated Bibles and Bible commentaries give ample room to questions of historical setting, author, genre, and the like. An agrarian homiletic affirms all of this, and it also seeks to go deeper. It begins by insisting that no place or time is just like any other, and any attempt to speak on behalf of the other—especially an other separated by vast times and distances—bespeaks an unconscious or uncaring triumphalism. It is risky enough to make a claim about "what Isaiah meant" or "what Jesus is saying here"; how much more if the claim is not informed by a deep effort to see the primary material in as many contexts as possible, to recognize that we are not standing on the shoulders of Scripture in order to see further but are sitting at its feet in the posture of a student. That this effort will inevitably be partial and partly a failure is, for the agrarian, neither a surprise nor a cause to abandon the effort.

For the agrarian the goal of contextual reading is to celebrate and explore the way each book, author, person, group, and event speaks their own word in their own time. The agrarian is not troubled by scriptural diversity or even by scriptural disagreements. Rather than asking all of Scripture to tell a predetermined story—one that inevitably reflects the exegete's perspectives and biases—the agrarian asks the different parts of Scripture to tell the stories they wish to tell. A commitment to see each person, each farm, each community as unique entails a similar commitment to Scripture.

Given what Berry has written about scale, limits, and the local, it should hardly be surprising that for the agrarian the principal gift of reading contextually is the ability to see the world "from below." If one wishes to look at Scripture from above—from a vantage of success or triumphalism or glory—one must stay with large claims and metanarratives. In such a case one will be tempted to recount the whole sweep of Scripture as the story of God and God's people moving from victory to victory—from creation in Genesis to victory over Egypt to the building of the temple to the Incarnation and the resurrection to the glories of the second coming of Christ. Or one will repeat nuanced stories in unnuanced ways: David as the paradigmatic king who rules over the United Monarchy, Elizabeth and Mary as model mothers through whom God works out Israel's salvation, Peter and Paul as the heroes of the early church who proclaim Christ fearlessly. This is the view of Scripture from thirty-thousand feet.

There is a bit of truth in all of these broad claims, just as an airplane at high altitude will be able to see some of the larger features of the land below. However, a commitment to context forces the exegete and the preacher to slow down, to see these narratives and individuals in more nuanced ways. Slowing down and looking for nuance inevitably yields distinctiveness within stories and differences among stories. Yes, David and Elizabeth and Mary and Peter and Paul all play archetypal roles: but even the archetypes get skewed when seen from a great height. How much more valuable to read David within the literary motifs of the historical books, to recognize that the authors of those books valued and even highlighted the complexity of David's long life, full as it was of victory and defeat, virtues and deep flaws. How important it is to read Luke's story of Elizabeth and Mary as truly radical: Luke asks us to see both women as people with profound prophetic and theological gifts to share. How crucial to read the Exodus and the stories of Christ's incarnation and resurrection as God's rescue of particular peoples. How illuminating to recognize that the Gospels, Acts, and the New Testament letters give us pictures of Peter and Paul as men often prone to failure and working out the implications of the Incarnation in situations of fear and uncertainty. These kinds of insights are available only to someone committed to reading Scripture from below.

An agrarian commitment to reading from below entails a willingness to read and preach prophetically. Partly such a willingness results from the insight that the prophets are at the center of scriptural reflections on the land, a land economy, and God's commitment to Israel and Judah as people of the land. At the most basic level, agrarian preachers will be concerned with whether the Old Testament texts with which they are working are pre-exilic, exilic, or post-exilic. Of even broader importance than the claim that the preacher ought to engage with the prophets of the Old Testament and the many prophetic voices of both testaments is the insight that prophetic speaking is at its core proclamation from below.

Prophets are radicals. They call people back to the roots of the movement. Israel's prophets rise to prominence in response to the rising ruling class: one thinks of Samuel's complex relationship with Saul, and of Nathan's with David. The words of Isaiah, Jeremiah, and all the rest of the prophets associated with their own books repeatedly call God's people back to their fundamental relationships and commitments to God, to the temple, to covenant, to the neighbor and the alien in their midst. Other prophetic voices—Mary in the Magnificat, Jesus in the Sermon on the Mount—do much the same. Mary emphasizes the overturning of triumphalist hierarchies: "He has brought down the powerful from their thrones, and lifted up the lowly; he has filled the hungry with good things, and sent the rich away empty" (Luke 1:52–53). Jesus blesses that which seems cursed—the poor, the meek, the grieving.

Much distinguishes these prophetic voices from each other, but what binds them are several of the themes central to the agrarian perspective. They are overwhelmingly interested in specifics—specific people, places, and circumstances. They believe that it is fundamental to God's nature to surprise and scandalize, to overturn that which is unjust and to establish that which is righteous. They are concerned with questions of membership, and they offer visions of membership that are both larger and less conventional than human visions. Finally, they are concerned with economics, and they believe that God is too: God's justice is not an abstraction but is literally a place on the land and food in the hand and fair treatment by the ruling powers. An agrarian preacher, then, must be similarly radical and similarly prophetic.

THEOLOGICAL CONTEXT

This is certainly not the place to rehearse earlier arguments elucidating the relationship between Luther's theology of the cross and Berry's agrarianism: it is probably sufficient to recall that both work by opposites and challenge our notions of meaning, reason, and scale. This is the place, however, to indicate how a theological commitment to the cross ought to inform agrarian preaching.

First, because Luther's theology of the cross requires us to see by opposites, we must preach in a way that perceives God in the midst of suffering. That is, the preacher of the cross does not try to persuade a congregation that the world is other than it is, nor that God can only be found in the parts of the world of which we approve. Rather, the cross insists that God is humble enough to dwell in the suffering of the world. Further, the agrarian preacher will want to be specific about suffering. It is not enough to speak generally of sin and death, or of grief and sorrow. The agrarian will highlight connections between biblical dislocations—slavery in Egypt, the exile, foreign occupation—and our dislocation from the land, from local communities, and from each other. The agrarian will insist that the suffering of the planet is of profound concern; as Berry writes, "Nature is party to all our deals and decisions, and she has more votes, a longer memory, and a sterner sense of justice than we do."[2] The agrarian will be bold about sources of suffering that mask themselves under the cloak of cultural approval or indifference: technophilia, consumerism, global corporations, and the like. Preaching God's presence in the midst of these forms of suffering (and many others) reveals the kind of God we have—one who is not afraid to dwell in both sacred and desecrated places.

Preaching into opposites entails a willingness to be surprised and to surprise the congregation. Preaching into suffering is one such form of surprise, but it is not the only. In addition, the preacher must be willing to preach scandalously, which is to say, preach bravely into the claim that the ways of God and the gospel of Jesus are a stumbling block not just to the skeptical but to believers. A willingness to scandalize is requisite if one is going to avoid the dualism so abhorrent to an agrarian theology. For example, in the season of Advent or Lent, preachers may well feel a call to indict the excesses of a consumer culture. However, preachers disinclined to trouble the waters will find themselves tempted to fall back onto one of two false dualisms (or both!)—between the culture and the church, or between the material and the spiritual. In the former case, timid preachers will lay the blame at the foot of the culture without acknowledging the church's inextricable economic links to that culture. In the latter case, timid preachers will encourage so-called spiritual practices—lighting candles, saying more prayers, cursing less, disavowing chocolate—which make us "better people" without actually calling us to change our earthly lives. The brave preacher, however, will proclaim just the opposite—to wit, we are bound body and soul to both culture and church; and real acts of repentance and discipleship begin with costly questions about our own complicity in falsehood.

Such a courage is a deep thorn in the side of reason, and troubling reason is also a central call of agrarian, cruciform preachers. The point is not that one cannot preach sermons that have a logical structure or that make points which the human mind can contemplate. Rather, just as the theology of the cross challenges our common-sense understanding of our relationship to God—that God rewards the good and punishes the evil and therefore our job is to live a life that somehow impresses our creator—so agrarianism challenges everyday understandings of the church. Where our

---

2. Part of an endorsement statement for *The Dying of the Trees* (1997) by Charles E. Little.

basic instinct is to succeed, agrarianism seeks instead to sustain; where our instinct is to church growth and a central place in the culture, agrarian preaching advocates flourishing in care and celebrates church in the margins. If such preaching troubles the congregation, the preacher is probably doing it right!

All of this really comes down to agrarian preaching as a challenge to the powers and principalities of this world. These powers have a hundred manifestations—multi-national corporations, rampant consumerism, environmental destruction, dualistic division between people and the sources of their food, and on and on. The important point, however, is that these are not simply forces "out there." Just as agrarian preachers cannot ignore these powers, neither are such preachers allowed simply to demonize them as forces that victimize us: the deeper truth is that they are us and we are them. Preaching against the powers begins by highlighting our own complicity and economic support of those very powers.

The challenge, then, is to preach towards an alternative way. Agrarianism cannot preach grace as though it were an abstract super-power that God possesses. Grace is not a magic wand. Rather, it is a transformative word of God. Not only does it find the lost, free the bound, and forgive the sinner, it sets us on a new and different path. Therefore, to challenge the powers—to preach the cross—is to lead people to see church in a new light. One of the most helpful ways to do this is to celebrate and encourage celebration of the small. More will be said on scale later on, but it is important here to be clear that both Luther's theology of the cross and an agrarian ecclesiology possess a fundamental bias away from the large, the triumphal, and the universal in favor of the small, the faithful, and the particular.

An example is illuminating. A great many American Christians look at mainline church buildings three-quarters empty on a Sunday morning and lament their loss of prominence, power, and people. In my own experience, I have heard long-time members bemoan a Christmas Eve service with only one hundred people when there used to be so many people that extra chairs were needed in a sanctuary that seats three hundred and fifty. The implied and sometimes explicit wish is that the congregation were large the way it used to be. From this point of view, the church of today invariably savors of anticlimax: no matter the ministries birthed or the people served, the church is smaller; and smaller is worse. An agrarian perspective, willing to scandalize our common sense, speaks the opposite word: the problem with these congregations is not that the communities are too small but that the buildings are too large. The buildings are sarcophagi of a triumphalist age; and all too often the people who use them are worshipping a past more troubling—more beholden to the powers and principalities—than anyone is able to admit. Such a preacher will be bold enough to say that the building and its concomitant drain on resources is no longer an ark but an anchor, and that a focus on the small—particular people, particular ministries— ought to compel us to abandon the building and retain the commitment to a surprising God.

ECONOMY

Much has already been written about the centrality of economy to an agrarian model of church. What remains to be elucidated is how a pastor or minister is to keep such matters before the congregation when preaching. There are probably an endless number of strategies for doing this, and different pastors will approach their congregations in their own unique way. This is precisely the kind of local variety that agrarians celebrate. Nonetheless, in light of Berry's understanding of agrarianism, a few suggestions seem especially pertinent. The first concerns Scripture, the second church finances, and the third the pastor's call to be a local presence in the community.

First, one way of remaining attuned to the economic, political, and agrarian issues is to highlight the centrality of these issues to Scripture. A preacher committed to this focus will work as much as possible with the original languages. There is no way around it: translations hide meaning and nuance. As the Italian adage has it, *Traduttore, traditore*. The phrase is appropriately slippery to translate, but is usually rendered, "To translate is to betray." A preacher who wants to engage Scripture for agrarian preaching needs to get to the original languages. Even if Hebrew and Greek are for many preachers now mostly dusty memories from seminary days, there are lexicons, interlinear Bibles, textual commentaries, and the like that allow for a more direct engagement.

Such a direct engagement with language helpfully resists various temptations, such as the temptation to treat all of Scripture as though it speaks with a single voice or the temptation to read so-called spiritual words—holy, glory, heaven, and others—in a triumphalist sense. Words like these are less amenable to a theology of glory when understood contextually and in their original tongue. For example, one of the Hebrew words for glory—*kabod* and its cognates—appears in dozens of passages in

Scripture, and it almost goes without saying that a theologian of glory will interpret those passages with an eye towards how the invisible God is made visible in honor and splendor. This is not precisely or entirely wrong. However, even someone with virtually no Hebrew will find in the lexicons and commentaries that *kabod* is etymologically related to the Hebrew word for heaviness or weightiness. The glory of the Lord in this sense might be said to be akin to gravity or gravitas. An agrarian preacher, then, will notice how often this kind of glory—what Paul will call "an eternal weight of glory" (2 Cor 4:17)—is said to descend or come down, how God's glory shows God coming into creation and not creation ascending into the divine. Further, such a preacher may well be provoked to think how God's descent in glory is a revelation that also conceals: the God who is revealed in cloud and fire and smoke is a mysterious God willing to show up in unexpected and even shocking places.

Two further examples, both from the New Testament Greek, will have to suffice to indicate the value of original languages to an agrarian preacher eager to think in economic terms. First, it is worth every preacher's time to be reminded again and again that the word "you" in the New Testament is routinely plural. Commands and promises alike are given most often to God's people as a corporate body—a crowd by the side of the sea, early church communities in urban centers, the people of God scattered across the world. The plural "you" is virtually impossible to render clearly into English without dipping into the colloquial—the southern "y'all," the Pennsylvania Dutch "youse." Yet how important it is when avoiding mere personal piety and recognizing that God's promises address the Great Economy.

A second example: many preachers—probably most—dread those Sundays when Jesus' teachings on divorce are central to the Gospel reading. The Scylla and Charybdis in such a case seems to be either singling out the divorced in the room for a public shaming or somehow trying to show that Jesus did not mean what he seems pretty clearly to be saying. And yet, at least in Matthew's version of this teaching, found in the Sermon on the Mount, a brief encounter with the Greek is helpful because it reveals the economics that undergird the teaching. Matt 5:31 is rendered by the New Revised Standard Version as "Whoever divorces his wife, let him give her a certificate of divorce." This is not a bad translation, and it wisely avoids hiding the socio-economic reality that until quite recently divorce was a legal proceeding that could only be initiated by the man. That is, it avoids decontextualizing the passage by translating "wife" as "spouse." Nonetheless, a direct encounter with the Greek will show that the phrase translated "Whoever divorces his wife" says in reality, "Whoever dismisses [*apolyse*] his wife." Further, the direct encounter will show that the word translated "certificate of divorce" [*apostasion*] has at its core "a standing-apart," that is, a legal standing separate from him. Such insights allow the careful preacher to see that what is being described and condemned is a particular kind of economic and legal cold-heartedness by which a faithful wife is left without the means of subsistence. Indeed, in the light of these insights, it would not be overreading to claim that Jesus' condemnation is aimed not at the wife, but at the husband: the Greek phrase often translated as "causes her to commit adultery" [*poiei auten moixeuthenai*] might just as well be translated "makes her" or even "forces her." The economic and legal issues are central; the moral status of divorce is barely secondary.

Many more examples could be adduced, beginning with uses of the word economy [*oikonomia*] itself; but these few must stand for the whole. The point being made is not a small one: Scripture is brimming with social, political, and economic implications from start to finish; and if we avoid seeing them, it is probably because it is convenient to our minds and less burdensome to our consciences to do so.

Two other strategies for preaching into the economics of agrarianism deserve attention. The first is simply to make the congregation's economic life a recurring theme in preaching. Far too many pastors avoid talking about money in their sermons; the annual stewardship sermon is the extent of their economic preaching, and even then it too often tends to be not much more than an exhortation to increase giving. Agrarian preachers, however, know that the congregation's genuine, though often unspoken, principles are reflected in how they spend money as well as how they give. The pulpit is an appropriate place to reflect on what is being spent locally versus what is being spent in support of the global economy. It is also an appropriate place to challenge situations where the congregation is investing in a theology of glory: why, for example, does a congregation struggling to develop ministry invest heavily in fixing the organ or re-leading old stained-glass windows?

Finally, the agrarian preacher ought to be sufficiently knowledgeable about the local community to be able to advocate for it and reflect on the congregation's place in it. Pastors who live a long commute away from their congregation will need to work extra hard, but pastors who live locally must put in the time and energy as well. Good agrarian preachers will have eaten in the local restaurants; they will shop locally and know the names of local craftspeople. They will keep an eye on the scores of the local schools' sports teams. They will help their congregation see themselves as part of a particular place within a particular economy, and they will praise the congregation that serves willingly in that place.

PLACE AND SCALE

Probably Berry's most frequent lament is that we have lost our connection to our places. His is not a mere nostalgia for a time when people lived on the same land as their forebears but rather a grief that people without a connection and commitment to place have lost far more than even know:

> To be disconnected from any actual landscape is to be, in the practical or economic sense, without a home. To have no country carefully and practically in mind is to be without a culture. In such a situation, culture becomes purposeless and arbitrary, dividing into "popular culture," determined by commerce, advertising, and fashion, and "high culture," which is either social affectation, displaced cultural memory, or the merely aesthetic pursuits of artists and art lovers.[3]

To be disconnected from landscape is to be without a home is to be without a culture is to be caught in the ebb and flow of ersatz cultures that are "purposeless and arbitrary." These losses are a dislocation of the profoundest kind if one believes—as Berry does (and as I do)—that human beings are hard-wired to thrive within relationship to God, to community, and to place.

It is prudent not to overstate what a congregation—even a congregation striving to live within an agrarian model—can accomplish in the face of all this. The simple truth is that against the financial might of overwhelming multi-national, national, and corporate juggernauts, the local congregation offers a set of protests that are largely prophetic and symbolic in nature. And if this kind of humility is appropriate for the congregation, it is even more so for the agrarian sermon. Just as preachers are not themselves defeating sin and death from the pulpit, so preachers are not going

3. Berry, *Citizenship Papers*, 86.

to overwhelm the forces of Walmart and Amazon, even with a lifetime of sermons.

Nonetheless, the preaching matters. The forces at work in our world may change slowly, but every effort to move them matters. The faithful preacher is proclaiming the gospel not simply in the presence of the current moment but in the face of an ever-encroaching eschaton. In the light of the Great Economy—the already-and-not-yet kingdom—the preacher needs to find a particular word for a particular people at a particular time. Their auditors need to be reminded that they are more than what current cultures and economies say they are.

In practical terms Leonora Tubbs Tisdale gives a great deal of sound advice to the preacher interested in local context. She believes deeply that "congregational preachers are also local theologians, called to craft theology that is shaped for very particular communities of faith."[4] As such she offers a series of hallmarks for the preacher of local theology. While I will not rehearse all of them, three stand out. Tisdale's first hallmark is this: "Preaching as *local* theology celebrates week-to-week congregational preaching, and the power of the particular in gospel proclamation."[5] This point might seem obvious, but it is not. Especially in a culture that insists on busyness as a marker of vocational value and that demands high levels of technology-driven connectedness—email, cell phone, text messaging, Facebook, etc.—it is an increasingly rare preacher who can make the time for a well-crafted sermon that strives to articulate a local theology. Even more rare is the congregation that understands the value and the difficulty of this kind of preaching and helps to protect a pastor's time and boundaries.

Pastors who are serious about articulating a local theology need to do several things. First, they need to fight against the implicit assumption that a church is a kind of business and that the pastor is a kind of CEO. This fight is made more difficult as churches continue to hold onto corporate models that may have worked well fifty or a hundred years ago but that are increasingly inefficient. Councils, committees, congregational meetings, and regular reports are just the tip of a corporate iceberg. Second, they need to "count as work" activities that are not strictly utilitarian: reading good books, keeping an eye on magazines and journals in fields other than their own, taking walks, tending a garden. Such activities ground the preacher

---

4. Tisdale, *Preaching as Local Theology and Folk Art*, 39.
5. Tisdale, *Preaching as Local Theology and Folk Art*, 40.

in their own community in ways that no corporate work ethic can compete with.

A second hallmark from Tisdale is this: "Preaching as *local* theology has as a goal the transformation of the imaginations of the hearers in accordance with the message of the gospel."[6] It is hard to imagine a claim closer to the heart of what Wendell Berry is striving to accomplish. Throughout all the genres in which he writes, he is aiming to stir the imagination of his readers. Through his fiction he invites them to imagine a time and place like our own but transformed by an agrarian vision. In his poetry he most often describes the agrarian life as he lives it, asking us to imagine ourselves into lives of similar obligation and joy. And in his essays he most often asks us to see the world in a new way, calling us to repent of the good that has been lost and to imagine a world redeemed of much that we have built. Both Tisdale and Berry offer the strongest of encouragements to the preacher: do not let your auditors believe that the life they are living is the only possible life or that the world that they see is the only possible world. Give them alternative images; imagine them into something they have yet to see. Agrarian preachers should, for example, push back whenever possible on the paucity of imagination that leads people to believe that eternal life is clouds and harps or that heaven is simply the American dream in its idealized state—an eternal game of golf (but without the bogies), an eternal theme park (but without the lines), an eternal road trip (but without the traffic). Again, they should offer a vision of people as something other than consumers and church communities as something other than private clubs.

Finally, Tisdale offers this: "In preaching as *local* theology, exegesis of the congregation and its subcultures is not peripheral to proclamation, but central to its concerns."[7] She recommends that preachers accomplish such exegesis by functioning like cultural anthropologists, existing as both insiders and outsiders within the community. There is a certain amount of common sense to this, and most preachers have had the experience of improved sermons as a concomitant of deepening relationships between preacher and congregation. From an agrarian point of view, we might push back a bit against the anthropologist model for fear that it overvalues professional expertise and distancing and undervalues relationship and shared commitments. We might nuance Tisdale's approach by asking what roles both preacher and congregation have in a community that functions

6. Tisdale, *Preaching as Local Theology and Folk Art*, 46.

7. Tisdale, *Preaching as Local Theology and Folk Art*, 48.

analogously to a farm or to a farming community. Scripture is a good place to search for such alternative models or roles.

It is tempting to move quickly to the idea that the preacher is the shepherd and the people are the flock of sheep. Except in fairly narrow circumstances, however, restraint must be used regarding this metaphor: while people actually living among sheep know them to be smarter and more complex than their reputation, for many Christians to be called a sheep is to be called witless and defenseless. It is far better to look in two other directions. First, the relation between preacher and congregation might be thought of as akin to the relation between farmer and farm hands. This is not a perfect metaphor: pastors do not own churches the way farmers own farms. And yet the relationship between the farmer and the farm hand is similar to what pastors and congregations have. The pastor is tasked with casting the vision, with seeing that all parts of a congregation are working in concert, and with overseeing central things—word and sacrament. The pastor is also well aware that the congregation does a majority of the work and that the ministry of the place is done well only if pastor and people share a vision. There is a respect and a love for the work and for each other that is crucial in both contexts.

One more helpful image is that of neighbor. This is both deeply biblical and fundamentally agrarian. It goes to the heart of Berry's idea of membership. It bespeaks the importance of place: neighbors are etymologically those who are nigh to us. Within a congregation it may also be aspirational: a congregation full of people who drive to church will need to work at genuine neighborliness. This difficulty, however, seems to me to make it all the more important for the agrarian preacher to preach into it. If we do not live on the same block or help each other bring in the crop, how do we make neighborliness a virtue among us, and how do we turn in meaningful ways to the neighborhood in which the church is physically located?

MEMBERSHIP

Much that has been said in other sections might be repeated here in a reflection on membership. Preaching that encourages a richer understanding of membership will point people to the cross; it will focus on economic practices; it will draw attention to the sacraments; and it will be concerned with issues of place and scale. Rather than rehearse such arguments, however, this section offers three suggestions for the preacher who wishes to develop an agrarian understanding of membership. Many others can, of course, be made.

First, agrarian preachers ought to aim for specificity—the good news in this time for these people. Such an approach shuns generalities and is wary of universal claims. Paradoxically, though, such preachers should be eager to introduce their auditors to the vast number of other Christian communities spread across time and space. Which is to say, agrarian preachers ought to be eager to share church history. People are more likely to see what is particular and valuable about their own community if they can begin to see the church universal in its ten-thousand local expressions. It is valuable to post-Christendom congregations to hear of Augustine and Hippo and the last days of the Roman Empire or of the struggles of nascent Christian communities on various frontiers or of communities that survived in hiding under one regime or another.

Second, agrarian preachers can deepen an awareness of membership by preaching regularly about financial stewardship. As Berry insists again and again, where we put our money tells the truth about what we believe. If our beliefs are not reflected in when and how we spend and save, then they are not really our beliefs at all. Thus, agrarian preachers ought to call their auditors to financial discipleship that reflects their place in the membership. This is precisely the opposite of "paying dues." Those who truly understand financial stewardship recognize that everything comes to us as a gift: our own economies are part and parcel of the Great Economy. All that we have been given, all we have earned, will "break free of [our] demanding and [our] praise."[8] Members need to be given new eyes, both for their own sake and for the sake of those their lives touch.

Finally, agrarian preachers should be enthusiastic about preaching within a lectionary. This might seem counterintuitive: would not a local community be better off choosing passages for their own needs? Perhaps this is so, and I would be curious to see how a well-led, well-read group of local Christians would locate ways of presenting both the Old and New Testament in rich, symphonic, trinitarian ways week after week, season after season. Nonetheless, the various lectionaries that currently exist—and especially the Revised Common Lection—go out of their way to do precisely the kinds of things an agrarian homiletic advocates: strong emphasis on creation, importance of local communities, prophecy in an exilic and post-exilic key, the quadrophonic witness of the Gospels honored in their

8. Berry, *Memory of Old Jack*, 192.

individuality, a keen interest in early Christian communities, and eschatology. Finally, a good lectionary brings the church into a cycle of seasons not unlike that of a farm. It is not that Advent, Lent, Easter, and all the rest mirror or shadow the seasons of the agrarian year. Rather the farm cycle of plant, grow, reap, and rest and the cycle of the church year remind us that we exist within pattern, within order. We are baptized into a membership; we are nurtured, loved, and mourned within that membership. We receive from the past, we strive to be faithful in our time, and then we pass on. The farm and the church tell a different story from the culture: ours is not the story of progress and endless growth; it is rather the story of faithfulness and fecundity. It is not the story of success but of good care.

SACRAMENTS

Wendell Berry is capable of writing about the creation in a sacramental way, though perhaps principally in the sense that nature is for him literally a holy thing, a sacred thing and a mystery. He can write poems like this:

> The dark around us, come
> Let us meet here together,
> Members one of another,
> Here in our holy room. . . .
> Light, leaf, food, hand, and wing,
> Such order as we know,
> One household, high and low,
> And all earth shall sing.[9]

The words are liturgical in their invocation of "Members one of another" and "our holy room." Berry is surely speaking of a forest—"Light, leaf, food, hand, and wing"—and also of something more than a forest. The forest participates in and stands for the Great Economy, the "household" or *oikonomia* that encompasses both "high and low." Further, by invoking words dear to the church as he does, he invites juxtaposition of outdoors and indoors, of a forest and a sanctuary.

Such a juxtaposition, it seems to me, should be regularly in the preacher's mind and manuscript, regularly presented to the gathered assembly. In that most indoors of places, the church building, bread and wine and water invite and perhaps even compel church members to participate

9. Berry, *This Day*, 47.

in what is outdoors—the field, the vine, the river. For sure this is how liturgical theologian Gordon Lathrop understands the sacramental elements.
He writes this of bread.

> The loaf draws us. It easily stands for the cooperation of human
> work with the land. . . . for the circle of shared eating. . . . Bread
> is never far from death. At the loaf we may know ourselves to be
> contingent beings, dependent on that which is outside us.[10]

And this of wine:

> The translucent liquid also holds together the fruitful earth, the
> sun and the rain, the ancient history of human cultivation. . . . It is
> meant for a group. . . . Here, poured out for a human circle, there
> flows the goodness of the earth pressed out, the sun made liquid.[11]

And finally this of water:

> All water is sacred, flowing from beyond here. . . . But the water is
> not tame. . . . If bread and wine are at the center of the assembly,
> water is at the edge, marking its boundary, slaking its thirst, hold-
> ing its life and death.[12]

Lathrop is poetic, but he is not merely (or even primarily) metaphorical.
Bread and wine actually enter our blood stream, that which was outdoors
becoming part of our own bodies. They are the result of sun and rain and
the labor of farmers. They feed us, and in our time and place we will feed
the earth with the bodies bread and wine have built. Water is nearly impossible to still. It gurgles and splashes; it passes into us, sustaining life, and
passes out of us, returning to the cycles of the world. The sacramental elements are both centripetal, drawing us together, and centrifugal, drawing
our attention to the larger membership of which this community is a part,
the membership of all creation.

    If all this is so—if the sacramental elements are polyvalent in ways that
call attention to the natural world, the outdoor and untamed world—then
why must the sacraments be preached? Is it not enough that they be expe-
rienced as water on the head or food and drink for the body? It is a good
question. Luther addressed it nearly five-hundred years ago when he wrote
"Baptism is not simply plain water. Instead, it is water used according to

10. Lathrop, *Holy Things*, 91.
11. Lathrop, *Holy Things*, 92.
12. Lathrop, *Holy Things*, 94–95.

God's command and connected with God's Word."[13] And again "Eating and drinking certainly do not do [such great things], but rather the words that are recorded: 'given for you' and 'shed for you.'"[14] To put it simply, the words matter. Even as the sacraments themselves draw people into relationship with God and then remind them over and over of what that relationship means, so preaching is an act of remembering and reminding; and it is appropriate to draw the hearts and minds of the auditors to the elements. It is appropriate both to remind them of the rich meaning found in food and drink and also to deepen their understanding of it. Such meaning certainly seems to be in Berry's mind when he quotes another poet:

> When I think of the meaning of food, I always remember these lines by the poet William Carlos Williams, which seem to me merely honest:
>
>> "There is nothing to eat
>> seek it where you will,
>>   but of the body of the Lord."[15]

TECHNOLOGICAL SKEPTICISM

Technological skepticism is a concomitant of much that has already been written—concern for creation, antagonism towards industrialism, and matters of economy, to name but a few. Yet it is often difficult to get contemporary Christians, even those with agrarian sympathies, to wrestle critically with the value and expense of technology. This struggle is well-illustrated by a brief story. Many years ago, when I was a high school teacher, the school where I taught made the decision that all students would be required to purchase laptops and carry them to their classes. While teachers were not absolutely required to employ said laptops in the classroom, a host of seminars, all-day forums, and faculty meetings exerted significant cultural and professional pressure on teachers to make sure they did not "fall behind." Questions about financial cost, weight, relative usefulness, and opportunities for misuse were all swept aside.

Because I had seen laptops do genuine damage to English classrooms at other schools, I made an appointment to speak with a senior administrator

13. Luther, *Contemporary Translation of Luther's Small Catechism*, 41.
14. Luther, *Contemporary Translation of Luther's Small Catechism*, 50.
15. Berry, *What Are People For?*, 152.

about my concerns. The outcome was of course foreordained. My Luddite demur did not deflect the trajectory of a program designed to polish the school's reputation and keep the students up to date in a technophile culture. What interests me here is not the outcome but the response I received. In the midst of a conversation in which I argued along lines I would learn to call agrarian—decrying the loss of face-to-face discussion, pointing out the certainty that students would "multi-task" in class by checking email and surfing the web, arguing that the heart of the classroom is relationship and knowledge rather than data—I was brought up short by the person across the table. "Can we at least agree," the administrator asked, "that technology itself is a neutral tool?" I was, frankly, stunned by the obtuseness of the question.

Technology is never neutral. It makes some things obsolete; it makes other things more important. It creates some jobs while eliminating others. It improves some aspects of life and worsens others. It changes what it encounters. None of this is neutral. There are, therefore, real issues that need to be addressed in the face of technological change. These issues might be posed as a series of related questions. What is the actual value of the supposed benefits, and do those benefits outweigh the negative effects? How do we make a full reckoning of the price to be paid, and how will we measure that which is precious but not quantifiable? Who will gain from the new technology, and who will lose; what price will be paid by all affected? Other questions might well be added, but even these few indicate the paucity of reflections that attends the adoption of most new technologies.

Automobiles are a good example. A simplistic understanding of this technology is that it improves the speed and reliability of transportation and has therefore improved our lives. A fuller understanding would have to take much more into account. It would ask, for example, what the cost is to the earth in terms of mining, production, and pollution. It would ask how automobiles have shaped the lives of those who cannot live without cars and the lives of those who cannot afford cars; it would ask how cars have transformed the lives of communities. It would even stretch and ask larger questions about public policy, about the decline of public transportation, about the rise of multi-national corporations, and so on. As a world wrestling with climate change is coming to realize, a failure to reckon with the full effects of technological changes does not prevent the effects from occurring. On the contrary, such a failure of insight and imagination inevitably compounds the price to be paid down the road.

All of this matters to the agrarian preacher for several reasons. First and most directly, preachers in North America are almost certainly preaching to congregations of technological addicts. The vast majority of their church members are spending hours and hours a day in front of televisions, computers, phones, and various other screens; they are spending large sums of money to acquire and maintain the most recent technological "advances"; and they are increasingly tracked and marketed to with pinpoint accuracy by a data-driven, corporate-driven culture. If this does not cause Christians to pause and reflect, then they are far gone indeed.

Further, what is true of individual members is also true of congregations themselves. They are building websites, making sure they maintain a high profile online, and purchasing high-tech security systems. In homes and churches, cameras and sensors are increasingly common. We have become volunteers in a culture that feeds our fears and then offers to sell us technology to assuage it. Even George Orwell could not have imagined a situation in which Big Brother is watching, not because we cannot prevent him, but because we ourselves paid a company to come in and install his cameras. Freedom is slavery, indeed!

Agrarian preachers need to tell the truth about this. They need to point out that much that is of value within the church—the emphasis on communal gatherings, its insistence on touch (the handshake, the hug, the bread eaten and the wine drunk), its assurance that we are not to be afraid—is undercut by the cultural love of technology. When members itch to put up screens in the sanctuary to attract young people, when congregations claim to be "doing church" online, when large sums of the budget are given over to technology without asking the larger questions about cost and benefit, the agrarian preacher needs to step into the gap and remind the community of the true gifts of the church: the word preached, the meal eaten, the ministry carried out in the world.

This is hard to do. Far too many people within the church are just like the school administrator of whom I wrote: they cannot imagine technology as anything but a neutral tool. Indeed, they are more likely to see it as a profoundly useful tool, dismissing the many costs as incidental to the unquestioned benefits. And this difficulty in seeing the issue is the other, larger reason that the agrarian preacher must speak: because people do not recognize their own addiction, they cannot hear—cannot comprehend—that the love of technology is a form of triumphalism, even a theology of glory. It claims to give meaning through visible—indeed, purchasable—markers.

Even more, it routinely claims that those who oppose technological triumphalism are troglodytes, Luddites, medievalists in the worst sense, people who would take us back to a time before modern medicine and cappuccino machines.

Agrarian preachers need to call out triumphalism wherever they see it and even when such a call is unpopular. They need to say honestly that Americans, and especially affluent white Americans, are devouring the earth's resources all out of proportion to their numbers. They need to say that most forms of contemporary technology are not good for you: they will not make you happy, they will not bring you closer to human community and family, and for sure they will not deepen your relationship to God or God's creation.

ESCHATOLOGY

It would be easy either to overstate or to understate the role of eschatology in agrarian preaching. Easy to overstate because, while eschatology is a crucial element of preaching, eschatological passages need not be central week in and week out. Indeed, such centrality runs the real risk of endorsing in worship a dualism focused on the heavenly at the expense of the earthly. Easy to understate because agrarianism's focus on land and location can make it easy to conceive agrarianism as mere ruralism. Focusing on the gifts of creation, one can slip into an unbalanced emphasis on particular economic issues and social causes in the present. Such an approach falls into a dualism that focuses on the earthly at the expense of the heavenly.

The tendency to remember the earth and forget the heavens—or vice versa—points to why eschatology is so important to true agrarian preaching: it is the job of the preacher to speak of the marriage of heaven and earth, mind and body, creation and new creation. Agrarian preachers are called again and again to draw their auditors into an increasing awareness of their interrelatedness to the rest of the Great Economy and to God's redemptive work in, through, and beyond time. This interrelatedness comes to a climax in eschatology for the agrarian because only in the fullness of time is there a full harvest of God's intentions.

A passage from *The Memory of Old Jack* is instructive. The protagonist, Jack Beechum, is at pains to show the importance of limits and boundaries to a younger farmer, Matt Feltner. Berry writes of the two men looking out over the Kentucky landscape:

Jack would gesture with his hand to the ridges and hollows that bore indelibly for them both the memory and the mark of Ben, and he would say: "That's all you've got, Mat. It's your only choice. It's all you can have; whatever you try to gain somewhere else, you'll lose here." And then, taking hold of Mat's shoulder, letting him see in his eyes with what fear and joy he meant it, he would say: "And it's enough. It's more than enough."[16]

Such a passage might seem to militate against an eschatological reading of agrarianism: does not Jack indicate that the land alone is enough? In fact, he does not. On the contrary, he is pointing not to the land alone but to the land and the relationships among those who farm it, to the land and to the past and present, to the land and the gift of membership it makes possible. The land is marked for both of them by the memory of a beloved farmer now dead, Ben Feltner. Those earlier relationships with Ben are the crucible for their relationship to each other, to the land as locus of fear and joy, and to those who will come after them. The desire to "gain somewhere else" means only that "you'll lose here." We see here a principle dear to Berry's heart and near to the heart of eschatology: we see the eternal through the particular; only by entering fully into our particular place can we participate in the Great Economy of God.

To preach eschatologically is to assure a community that, all appearances to the contrary, what God is giving them in community together is "enough . . . more than enough." They have been brought together by those who have come before, and their meaning is tied up with those who will come after. To look for enduring meaning elsewhere than in God's Great Economy is to lose what has been given.

Thus eschatological agrarian preaching is biblical at least in the sense that it is grounded in the belief that God has made the world through love. The gift of land to Israel and the gift of particular communities to church and synagogue alike bespeak a God who does not abandon the creation. It is surely noteworthy in this regard that Revelation, the most relentlessly eschatological of biblical books, is unreservedly concerned with how God's judgment and salvation will finally come down to earth. Agrarian eschatological preaching is similarly focused on membership, noting how rarely in Scripture God saves individuals but how often the *telos* of God's activity is all humanity: "For God so loved the world" (John 3:16).

16. Berry, *Memory of Old Jack*, 163.

Eschatology may also give the agrarian preacher much needed courage, especially in the face of apparently indomitable economies and technologies. Agrarian preachers may take more than comfort in the assurance that destructive human economies will not have the last word. For if, as both Scripture and agrarians claim, God loves the creation and is intent on renewing it, then human economies can hope for no more than pale participation in the economy of God and are right when they fear that God's response to what we have sown is wrath. So, too, with technology. We are so used to the space it takes up in our lives that it is probably literally impossible to picture life without it. The eschatological agrarian, however, will rightly insist that God can and does picture it. I may be hopelessly naïve, but I do not imagine that a competent preacher will have a hard time assuring a congregation that cell phones, laptops, selfies, and the like are not integral to God's redemptive purposes.

Finally, the agrarian committed to preaching eschatologically will be drawn to preach on the sacraments in ways that bring together not only heaven and earth but also past and present with future. That the sacraments connect us to the past is perhaps obvious: they are instituted by Jesus and developed by the church in and through time. Baptism is participation in the membership of all those who have gone before; communion connects us both to the ongoing command of Jesus to "do this" and to the thousands—millions—of other times in which we and other Christians have gathered around bread and wine. That the sacraments connect us eschatologically to what is yet to come is less intuitive. The agrarian preacher draws us into this understanding by showing first that we are connected to those who come after us as surely as to those who have gone before: the membership works in both directions. Further, the elements themselves draw us into the creation—to fields and vineyards and rivers—and hence into the assurance that it is God's intention to redeem all the creation. We might put it this way: agrarianism without eschatology is mere nostalgia for an apparently simpler past, but agrarianism with eschatology is the announcement that the Great Economy of God will be victorious.

PATTERN

It might seem that this book is winding to a conclusion. A great many of Berry's central concerns have been molded into an ecclesiastical model and then propounded as pillars of an agrarian homiletic. One more issue needs to be addressed, however, one that is not always seen as central to the matter or material of a sermon but that is vital to the process of shaping and preaching an agrarian sermon. Pattern or structure is the final issue, in particular the pattern or patterns of preaching that are most fruitful for agrarian proclamation. This issue cannot be avoided because Berry himself has made patterns, especially narrative patterns, such a significant part of his own writing. He is at heart a storyteller. Though he writes comfortably in three genres—fiction, non-fiction essay, and poetry—he is never far from narrative. Even when he is not writing a novel or short story, stories are present in the text or are implicit behind it.

Berry's fondness for narrative—the integral role it plays in multiple genres—is a great gift for agrarian preachers, for by it they are reminded that their preaching needs to engage their listeners in ways that draw them into several interrelated narratives: the story of the congregation and its members; the story of the congregation within the larger church; the story of the church within the context of the Kingdom of God or the Great Economy. At the simplest level this means that, like Berry, preachers ought to allow a bit of poetry into their sermonic prose; they ought to be mindful that word choice is a part of performance. At a deeper level, though, Berry's use of narrative ought to lead agrarian preachers to a fuller appreciation for narrative and narrative structure in their own preaching. Like Berry, their prose ought to serve as a vehicle for getting their auditors to live into a more expansive worldview through imaginative sympathy with character and situation. Another way to say this is to insist that preachers must do more than argue along agrarian lines or exegete Scripture in ways that are faithful to an agrarian hermeneutic: they must tell the story of God's Great Economy in such a way that their auditors can imagine themselves in it.

There are literally dozens of models for preaching, and probably most of them could be employed by an agrarian preacher. Among the more common contemporary models of preaching, three seem to me to be especially well-suited to preaching in response to Berry's narrative understanding of the Great Economy: Paul Scott Wilson's four-page sermon, what Ronald J. Allen calls the "Sermon Developed as an Author Develops a Novel,"[17] and Eugene Lowry's homiletical plot. Each of these takes narrative seriously; Lowry's is probably the most helpful when responding to Berry.

Paul Scott Wilson's four-page sermon is well enough known not to need an extensive explication. In *The Four Pages of the Sermon: A Guide to*

17. Allen, "Sermon Developed as an Author Develops a Novel," 117.

Biblical Preaching, he identifies the four pages or moves as Trouble in the Bible, Trouble in the World, God's Action in the Bible, God's Action in the World.[18] That is, the first page or movement speaks about the theological troubles in the scriptural passage at hand; the second page moves directly or analogously from the troubles of the passage to the troubles we find in individuals, congregations, churches, and the whole world; the third page is a pivot to God's gracious response to the troubles in the passage at hand; the fourth page moves directly or analogously from God's grace in the passage to God's grace in the world. This approach has several elements to recommend it to an agrarian preacher.

First, Wilson's approach has much in common with Luther's emphasis on law and gospel. It insists that all of Scripture—and not only legal passages or passages of joy—reflect and illuminate both law and gospel, both trouble and grace. As such, the four-page sermon is resistant to a theology of glory. The very nature of the approach is that trouble is found at the center of the human experience and grace is understood as God's consistent—and consistently surprising—response to human trouble. A faithful preacher of this approach will be tempted neither by human accomplishment nor by an image of a vengeful or ruthless God. Rather, this approach rewards both the theologian of the cross and the mad farmer (or mad preacher!) who looks for hope in places other than power, success, growth, and the like.

A second way in which Wilson's approach is conducive to agrarianism is in its desire to stay rooted to the real world of the text and the real world of our lives. As was shown earlier, agrarian concerns and perspectives are part and parcel of the scriptural world and worldview. Creation is the act of a loving God; the land is a gift and also a central measure of covenant relation between God and God's people. Jesus is rooted in a Jewish understanding of these gifts as shown through his deeds and his teachings—especially in the parables full of agrarian perspectives. To the extent that preachers take the Bible's agrarianism seriously in their preaching, they will find that both the troubles and the grace of the text elucidate agrarian perspectives. As to the world in which we live, Berry has been repeatedly clear that agrarianism is not synonymous with ruralism. Everyone who eats—that is, everyone—has a stake in land and land stewardship. As Berry writes, "Eating is an agricultural act."[19] Other reasons could be adduced, but these two make clear the value to the agrarian preacher of Wilson's approach.

18. Wilson, *Four Pages of the Sermon*.
19. Berry, *What Are People For?*, 145.

Another approach that is applicable to Berry's form of agrarianism is Allen's development of a sermon as an author develops plot. As Allen notes, this approach is able to "identify a way of preparing a sermon more than a pattern of movement in the sermon itself, or a distinctive focus on the subject, or a theological conviction."[20] That is, preachers employing this approach will concern themselves "with ideas and feelings about setting, characters, ethos, and plot."[21] Such a set of concerns is compatible with agrarianism because it too takes seriously the particulars of story. An agrarian exegete will not be strip-mining biblical texts for eternal truths, but rather reading Scripture responsive to its particular stories and patterns. Further, such an exegete will understand the local congregation as living out their own part in the larger story, the story of the kingdom or of God's Great Economy. Allen's further point about this approach also jibes well with agrarianism: "But as the author begins to write the novel, a strange thing happens. In a sense, the novel begins to write itself. . . . The plot begins to take on a life of its own."[22] Just so, the preacher who is responsive to a triple context—life of the text, life of the congregation, life of the preacher—will find the sermon moving in ways and directions that the preacher had not anticipated. Such movements are to be rejoiced in even though they may be unsettling. It is the given life and not the planned life that awakens the farmer's and the preacher's deepest joy.

For several reasons Eugene Lowry's understanding of the sermon as a narrative with a clear plot shows the greatest *prima facie* promise. First, like the four-page sermon, the narrative model is resistant to the preacher of glory. Such resistance is the result of the often overlooked truth that the story of glory is fundamentally dull and difficult to sustain as narrative. It is dull because, even when factually accurate in a superficial way, its focus on success, growth, size, and the like, cannot plumb the depths or illuminate the particularities of human experience. There have certainly been times and places when and where the church has grown and enjoyed success in such worldly fields as politics, education, and architecture. Much of the early middle ages in the West contains elements of such a story. Even in such times, though, the real interest is not to be found in the size or the scale but in the complex lives of the people and communities who lived in those times. I recognize that this point is not demonstrable as a fact, but it

20. Allen, "Sermon Developed as an Author Develops a Plot," 117.

21. Allen, "Sermon Developed as an Author Develops a Plot," 117.

22. Allen, "Sermon Developed as an Author Develops a Plot," 117.

seems to me little more than common sense that the varied experiences of
Francis, Aquinas, Abelard and Heloise, and the people they interacted with
(to name just a few) are of more genuine human interest than any argument
for the power and prestige of the church in that age.

Second and conversely, narrative preaching is conducive to a theology
of the cross. This is especially true because a preacher of the cross is committed to telling the truth, that is, to describing the world as it truly is. Such
a truth includes first what Lutherans call the law and what Wilson calls the
troubles in text and world. Further, a preacher of the cross is convinced
that stories that begin in truth and trouble and law end someplace very
different—namely, in grace and gospel. This is not to say that they end in
success or victory. A narrative preacher, like a theologian of the cross, can
see that even such a worldly defeat as a sacrificial death may be understood
as a revelation of God and of grace and of gospel. All of this is clearly useful
material for the agrarian preacher who is attentive to narrative.

A third reason to seek to ally agrarianism with narrative homiletics
will take longer to elucidate because it is grounded specifically in the relationship between the homiletical approach of Eugene Lowry and the short
fiction of Wendell Berry. In its simplest form, the relationship might be
stated thus: just as Lowry's narrative approach is essentially an argument for
writing sermons modeled on the pattern of a short story, so Berry's short
stories provide ample material for seeing how a narrative sermon might
draw on and reflect agrarian commitments. This is a rather large claim.

Lowry's homiletical plot has five steps or moves,[23] and each of these
also has a casual, short-hand term by which to identify them. The first step,
"upsetting the equilibrium," is known as "oops"; the second step, "analyzing
the discrepancy," is known as "ugh"; the third step, "disclosing the clue to
resolution," is known as "aha"; the fourth step, "experiencing the gospel," is
known as "whee"; the fifth step, "anticipating the consequences," is known
as "yeah." This pattern takes seriously that a faithful sermon is not simply
a discourse or a speech; rather, it reflects on and develops the narrative
tension that is part of both the Scriptures and the life of a Christian community. In other words, it sees story as central to Christian writings and life
and so intends to proclaim the gospel in a way that is also narrative.

Such an approach seems to me a helpful one. And yet I feel compelled
to offer a caveat: in many ways Lowry has presented in a more complex way
precisely the pattern of narrative that I ladled out to fourteen-year-olds in

---

23. Lowry, *Homiletical Plot, Expanded Edition*, 27–88.

the freshman high school English classes I taught for two decades. Within a few weeks of learning the pattern, these young people could readily unpack a short story in terms of (1) initial incident, (2) rising action, (3) turning point, (4) climax, and (5) resolution. While Lowry's vocabulary and explication of method are of course more sophisticated, the relationship between his idea of homiletical plot and the five parts of a short story is one of identity and not mere similarity. This is not to say that Lowry has not provided a helpful set of insights; on the contrary, he has made explicit a pattern and a commitment to narrative tension from which most good preachers can learn. It is, however, to say that viewing Berry's short stories as a homiletical resource is not a strained effort to forge connections across disciplines but is instead an effort at binocular vision—seeing Berry's agrarianism more clearly through Lowry's homiletical pattern and envisaging a sermon written in the Lowry pattern through the art of Berry's narrative.

Berry has written dozens of short stories, and analyzing or employing all of them is beyond the scope of these pages. However, it is possible to point to one that reflects patterns and concerns consistently present throughout Berry's fiction, to investigate it thorough Lowry's lens, and to see how its pattern provides insights for preachers. The story "Thicker Than Liquor" is set in the fictional town of Port Williams in 1930. Its plot follows the basic pattern of a short story. The story begins with Wheeler Catlett sitting in his small office in Hargrave, Kentucky. He is a newlywed, and he is just beginning to make a little money and make a few plans: "He was thinking about a home of his own, a place of his own. He liked his thoughts—which were, in fact, visions of Bess as happy as she deserved to be."[24] His thoughts are interrupted by a phone call telling him that his Uncle Peach is in a dive hotel in Louisville, drunk and unable to pay his bill. This is the initial incident—Lowry's "upsetting the equilibrium"—and it sends Wheeler into the rest of the narrative. He travels to Louisville, gets Peach cleaned up, and brings him home by train. His travel both to and from Louisville constitute the rising action or "analyzing the discrepancy." At any number of points Wheeler rejects the idea of turning his back on his troublesome uncle, and the reader learns the back story of Uncle Peach's alcoholism and the support he has received from Wheeler's parents.[25] The

24. Berry, *Wild Birds*, 4.

25. It is worth noting here that Berry uses the back story as a way of illuminating with nearly eschatological import the virtues and gifts of an agrarian life. In a scene as visionary as those of Jack Beechum and Jayber Crow, Wheeler sits with his father on the edge of a wagon bed after a hard day's work, the father impressing upon his son the sense of

turning point or "disclosing the clue to resolution" comes in a brief section in which Peach insists on fetching his horse and buggy and then vomits over and over as Wheeler drives him to Peach's house. This is both a literal turning ("Wheeler turned them to walk to his car, only to feel Uncle Peach turn in the opposite direction, a difference of intention that came close to bringing them both down"[26]) and also the cause of Wheeler's relational turning. He declares, "I hope you puke your damned guts out," and when Peach moans in reply, "Oh, Lord, honey, you can't mean that,"[27] Wheeler relents: "He put his arm around Uncle Peach, then, and patted him as if he were a child. 'No,' he said, 'I don't mean it.'"[28]

The climax—"experiencing the Gospel"—comes as the two men return to the farm. Wheeler hunts up some eggs from the barnyard, starts a fire in the stove, changes Peach's clothes and the bed linens, feeds his uncle, and puts him to bed. The sense of homecoming is made complete by Wheeler lying down next to his Uncle as his struggles with bad dreams and his addiction through the night. When Peach says, "Wheeler boy, this is a hell of a way for a young man just married to have to pass the night,"[29] we know he is right, but we have also learned that Wheeler will not abandon his uncle: "Later, Wheeler himself went to sleep, his hand remaining on Uncle Peach's shoulder where it had come to rest. And that is where daylight found him, far from home."[30] This is the resolution of the story; Wheeler's enacted love confirms the story's title—blood is indeed thicker than liquor—and fulfills Lowry's idea of "anticipating the future" by showing us the kind of man Wheeler is becoming.

There is no one-to-one correspondence between a short story and a sermon. It is not possible to present all or even much of "Thicker Than Liquor" in a sermon; and reading it from a pulpit might be instructive, but it would not be a sermon. Nonetheless, the agrarian preacher can learn

---

both time and timelessness that he experiences: "Marce Catlett sat looking at his son with a light in his eye that came from another direction entirely, waiting to see if [Wheeler] saw. It was a moment that would live with Wheeler for the rest of his life, for he saw his father then as he had at last grown old enough to see him, not only as he declared himself, but as he was. And in that seeing Wheeler became aware of a pattern, that his father both embodied and was embodied in" (Berry, *Wild Birds*, 11).

26. Berry, *Wild Birds*, 23.
27. Berry, *Wild Birds*, 23.
28. Berry, *Wild Birds*, 24.
29. Berry, *Wild Birds*, 26.
30. Berry, *Wild Birds*, 26.

from "Thicker Than Liquor" as well as from other Berry stories. The commitments and perspectives that undergird this story and that are expressed in its structure are fit to be translated or interpreted for use in the agrarian sermon.

Thus the initial incident introduces a local community, a character's economic hopes, and the inevitable brokenness that exists within any membership, even a close-knit family. The rising action or discrepancy encourages the preacher to analyze problems from a wide range of perspectives: Peach is a problem because he is family, because there is no fixing him, and because there is no abandoning him.[31] Agrarian preachers need to help their auditors recognize that our problems are deep-seated and cannot be fixed by any one of us working alone. Indeed, even together not all problems are fixable.

The turning point is wonderfully instructive: Wheeler can only address the problem by becoming more deeply involved in it and by seeing it through. Once he sees something childlike in his uncle's many failings ("he . . . patted him as if he were a child"[32]), he cannot sustain his anger. In Berry's terminology, he will not deny that they are both a part of the membership. The instruction for all preachers is that a true homiletic turning point must be as rich and as richly expressed as the problem it is addressing. It is irresponsible to wound the congregation with the troubles of the world and then give them a turning point no more healing or substantial than a simple assertion like "God loves you." Rather, the good news—the saving work of God as seen in Scripture and the world—must be explored and presented thoroughly.

The climax takes the agrarian preacher to the heart of the matter. In the return of Wheeler and Peach to the farm, Berry enacts the Parable of the Prodigal Son in another key: the Parable of the Alcoholic Uncle. Wheeler is akin to the generous father, forbearing from judgment, paying for all, and providing a meal. It is not going too far to say that he also acts for the same reasons as the generous father—because "this brother of yours was dead and is alive," because "blood is thicker than liquor." The resolution bespeaks

31. This section of the story also illustrates one of Berry's underrated gifts, a gift preachers would do well to cultivate as well—quiet humor. As Wheeler and Peach are riding the train home, Peach begins to vomit violently in a full train. Berry describes it by saying that, to "Wheeler, it was endurable only because it was inescapable . . . It would make a good story, as soon as he could get out of it. But it was not funny now" (Berry, *Wild Birds*, 22).

32. Berry, *Wild Birds*, 24.

the price paid by the one who will not abandon the beloved: Peach is redeemed, yet again, not with money alone, but by the willingness of the one who loves to give his body and his time and his money, the one willing not only to rescue the lost but to go into the darkness and abide with him there.

Other stories by Berry would highlight other agrarian themes and offer other insights for an agrarian sermon. The purpose of this close reading of "Thicker Than Liquor" is not to be comprehensive but to indicate a way for preachers to read short fiction as a tool for their preaching and as a resource for thinking structurally about sermon-writing. Indeed, this entire section on patterns is not so much directive as suggestive. By taking structure seriously—either in Wilson's four-page sermon or in a more explicitly narrative pattern—the agrarian preacher strives to challenge and nourish the imagination of auditors for whom agrarian ways of thought are largely foreign or forgotten.

6

The Agrarian Sermon—A Test Case

IT IS DIFFICULT TO quantify or even to track how the effort to think and preach as an agrarian changes someone engaged in the regular task of sermon-writing. The changes would be both small and large, profound at the level of both detail and worldview; and they would doubtless occur over time. The difficulty is compounded by the fact that there are few preachers explicitly engaging with these materials in a comprehensive way. I know pastors and preachers who have read some of Wendell Berry's writings or who have sympathies that align themselves with his central themes, but even they are generally using his ideas piecemeal and often in support of other interests. And while it might prove interesting to survey clergy or to track down preachers with agrarian concerns, Berry is probably right when he declares that he hears precious little from Christian pulpits that gives him hope. It is better for a single sermon to serve as a kind of test case or model and then for preachers to experiment on their own along agrarian lines.

A key advantage of discerning the utility of the agrarian model through one of my own sermons is that it acknowledges the inevitably autobiographical nature of this volume. Lurking not very far behind all that has been written here is a hope: these are approaches that I want to employ in my own ministry and that I believe help to shape a more faithful preacher. This is what I aspire to. Though the writing is formal, the goals are neither dispassionate nor impersonal.

The second advantage involves this particular sermon, written for Epiphany Sunday. It provides a nearly ideal test case because it was written in the midst of crafting this book but was not written as a response to it. That is, the mind that produced it was in the middle of reflection on agrarian homiletics, but the sermon itself was written for the worshipping community I shepherded at the time. It is not an effort to shoehorn itself into a set of agrarian claims or benchmarks. It was crafted with the same goal as the sermons from the Sunday before and the Sunday after, to wit, the proclamation of the gospel to the people of God in a particular time and place. Indeed, its usefulness for these pages did not occur to me until after it was preached: it is no more and no less than the most recent sermon I had preached when I began to realize the need for an example sermon.

Finally, the advantage of this particular sermon is that it cannot be considered a case of special pleading. The central text—Matthew's story of gentile magi come to worship the new Judean king—is not agrarian, agricultural, or rural in emphasis. It is neither a parable nor a prophecy that points in a straightforward way to issues of justice or economic equity. Exegetical insights or homiletical motifs typically drawn from it—as, for example, Jesus as light, the inclusion of the gentiles, the fulfillment of Old Testament prophecies in the life of Jesus—do not appear at first glance to be amenable to agrarian concerns. And yet, as I hope will be clearly seen, the agrarian perspective is capacious and thus capable of responding to this text in ways that are a faithful reflection of scriptural intent.

"THE SURPRISING STAR"

Surprisingly, the first words spoken by mortals in Matthew's Gospel come from the lips of the magi, these astrologer-astronomers from the east. They are star-gazers and they have seen a new star, rising in the East, and their question is a simple one: *Where is the one who has been born king of the Jews?* It ought to be an easy question to answer, but it is not. In one sense Matthew's entire Gospel is the story of different answers people offer to that question. Is it Herod the Great, the king living in Jerusalem at the time that the magi ask their question? Is it his son Herod Antipas, who figures so prominently in the deaths of John the Baptist and Jesus? Is it any of the various Caesars ruling from Rome?

Or is the King of the Jews none of these? Is it rather the child whom the magi finally meet at the end of their journey, the son of Mary to whom they give rare and exotic gifts? We have, of course, been given the answer in advance. Matthew spends the first chapter of his Gospel telling us the genealogy of this child—that is, his human origin—and then telling us of the angelic dream that Joseph has—that is, his divine origin. So there can be no doubt about the right answer. And yet Matthew also tells us the complicated story of the magi and their journeys so that we see how easy it is to miss the right answer. *Where is the one who has been born king of the Jews?* It ought to be an easy question, but it is not.

One of the reasons finding the true king is hard is that so many of the strongest candidates look alike. Herod the Great. Herod Antipas. Caesar Augustus. Caesar Tiberius. Of course they are all unique individuals with their own strengths and weaknesses. But they have more in common than they have differences. Their lives are about power, about ambition, about glory and making a name for themselves. They are all in the 1 percent, and they ultimately all seek to be rulers in the same kingdom—the kingdom of the world.

Let us not pretend that we are any different. We too define ourselves by power and prestige. We rejoice when our political party has a victory, and when the other party does well, we run around yelling that it is the end of the world and that they are traitors set on destroying this great nation. We fuel a global economy with barely a thought for what it's doing to the poor of the world or to the wonders of God's creation. We claim to care for our local community; we grieve when people don't support local businesses and struggling congregations; but then we pour tens of thousands of dollars into Target and Walmart and Amazon, corporations whose principal interest in Berks County is how to take money out of it.

O friends, do not doubt it. The kingdom of the world has a hundred ways of looking respectable. It calls itself "good business." It calls itself "being practical." It calls itself "the way things are." And the whole time it's hoping that we don't notice that there is a new star in the sky and that it is pointing not towards Jerusalem but towards the backwater town of Bethlehem.

The magi sure didn't realize this at first. They saw a star they had not noticed before, and it was in the part of the sky they associated with Judah. And so, of course, they headed to Jerusalem—to the capital and heart of the nation's power politics. Imagine their surprise when no son has been born to King Herod! Matthew's point is clear. The king whose coming is reflected by a new star in the heavens is not just any old king. He isn't just the latest ruler in the kingdom of the world. His coming will be both revealed and hidden. To answer the question of his birth, you have to be able to interpret the ancient Scriptures.

What the Scriptures in fact say is that Jerusalem is not the only city of David, that Bethlehem—the town of David's birth—also has a role to play. *And you, Bethlehem, in the land of Judah, [you] are by no means least among the rulers of Judah. For from you shall come a ruler who is to shepherd my people Israel.* This ancient prophecy about David is even more true of David's final great descendant, the child born in Bethlehem, the child whose lineage forms the core of Matthew's first chapter.

Again, Matthew's meaning is clear. Scripture leads us to a depth and an understanding of God's activity in the world in a way that no amount of star-gazing ever can. Yes, there are the stars above us and the moral law within us, and they point towards a creator both glorious and righteous. But the stars above and the law within cannot take us where Scripture can—to a God full of surprises. For who would have thought to look in Bethlehem? Who thinks *now* that the best way to see God in our world is to turn away from the bright lights of power and wealth and look in places of need and poverty and service?

There is one more step in the magi's journey, of course. They must get to Bethlehem and find the child. Much to their apparent surprise, the star begins acting less like a star and more like a GPS. It guides them to Bethlehem and then stops over the place where the child is. That is quite a star!

If Matthew has shown these magi, these gentiles, drawn to Bethlehem first by astrology and then by Scripture, what then is the meaning of this moving star in the final stage of the journey?

We begin to understand when we see how much this star acts like the angels who appear to the shepherds in Luke's story of Jesus' birth. The angels do two things, really. First, they give off light. They reflect the glory of God and assure those who see them that something big is going on in this apparently unimportant birth. And second, they give surprising guidance. They point the shepherds towards Bethlehem and tell them to look for a babe wrapped in bands of cloth. In other words, they take the shepherds and us to Jesus.

And that is what the star does, too. It gives off light, reflecting the glory of God and assuring us that something big is going on. And it guides the magi and us to Jesus. The light of the star guides us to the light of the world.

It is easy to get lost in the world. To set out with the best of intentions but find that the powers and principalities are lined up against us. The power-hungry want to rule us and abuse us. The greedy want to buy us, sell us, addict us and then make us pay through the nose for our addictions. There is a star to guide us, but how often our lives are cloudy. There are signs of God among us, but how often our hearts and minds are shrouded in mist. There are the Scriptures to point the way, but reading Scripture is hard work; how much easier to run our eyes over the endless babble of the daily paper and the internet.

All of this is why it matters so much that we gather here together week after week to reflect the light of Christ for each other. Hear me, friends: each of you reflects the light of Christ in your own unique way. When you are here, we see Christ in you in a way we cannot see in anyone else. And when you are not, we cannot see Christ in that way.

We can't make it alone, and we cannot make it without each other. To a world that isolates us and makes us feel alone—to a world that wants us to be nothing more than individual consumers—the gathered people of God respond with a resounding No! We have the light of Christ in our midst. We see it in each other's eyes. It is the light that makes wheat to grow and grapes to ripen on the vine. We *taste* the light. And, what is more, we *share* the light. We gather up the harvest of the earth and we send it out box after box, into home after home.

That great star on our wall is certainly meant to remind us of the Epiphany story we have in front of us today. The light that leads us. The glory of the Lord in our midst. Today let it also remind us of the cross that is hidden within it. Of the kingdom that the crucified one brings into our midst. The kingdom found in service and sacrifice. The kingdom that cannot be bought and cannot be sold . . . but that can be received by God's children as simply as bread in the hand and wine on the tongue; as light, warm upon the cheek and bright upon the eyes. Amen.

It must first be acknowledged that a single sermon cannot engage all agrarian concerns equally. For example, there is precious little eschatology in this sermon. What is more, while it is possible to discern a narrative pattern in this sermon,[1] I would say that it is too didactic to be understood as strictly narrative. Beyond that, however, this is an agrarian sermon through and through. It begins by taking seriously the historical and literary contexts in which Matthew is writing. It takes the time to reflect on what Matthew's audience would have understood magi to be, and it also delineates the key political players within the story and within the larger story Matthew is telling. Without making it central to the sermon, it takes seriously Matthew's pattern of leading gentiles first to Jerusalem and then—on advice of Jewish sages—to Bethlehem. It also addresses indirectly the odd way in which the star seems more like a character than a natural phenomenon within the story, pointing out how the star functions as a GPS and a guide not unlike the angels in Luke 2.

Theologically, this is a sermon written through the lens of the cross. It begins with the word "Surprisingly"; it takes the time to elucidate the many figures who would claim allegiance as the "true king" and contrasts

---

1. If I were asked to identify the five elements of a narrative pattern in this sermon, I would propose this: The first page offers the initial incident or difficulty: who is the proper king? The action rises as the community is included in those who are tempted by worldly candidates for our loyalty. The turning point is the recognition that the star guides the magi much as the angels guide the shepherds in Luke. The climax is the turn to the congregation as the place where we see Jesus. The resolution is the meaning of the large star on the wall and the invitation to the table.

them with Jesus; it highlights Bethlehem as the secondary city of David and points out how the star leads us away from the claims of power and prestige. It indicates that the light of Christ is seen most fully in another surprising place—the face of other Christians gathered for worship. Perhaps most significantly, it insists that Jesus' "coming will be both revealed and hidden." Finally, it calls on the congregation to recognize the cross within the star. At Advent Lutheran Church, the large star over the altar is probably twenty-five feet high: it dominates the altar wall of the sanctuary. That star has been for years the central image of the church; it has adorned envelopes and t-shirts and capital campaign literature. It has been an easy way to point to the light of Christ in a positive and non-dialectical way. Seen within that history, there is at least a dash of courage in the sermon's effort to point to what is clearly there but is easy to avoid—that the horizontal and vertical bars of the star form a cross. To point that out in the midst of this sermon is to complicate the congregation's image of itself. As the sermon says near its conclusion, "Today let [the star] also remind us of the cross that is hidden within it. Of the kingdom that the crucified one brings into our midst."

Probably the starkest way in which this sermon illuminates an agrarian approach is by its emphasis on economics and power. It is possible to write any number of sermons on this text without discussing economics; I know because I have both heard them and preached them. This sermon, however, roots itself in the claim that the question "Where is the one who has been born king?" is at its heart a political and economic question. It then takes the time to point out how much all the contenders for the title of true king have in common, and also how much we ourselves participate enthusiastically in the building up of earthly kingdoms that damage the earth itself and local communities everywhere.

The sermon also advocates for Berry's Great Economy by emphasizing local context, proper scale, and membership in contrast to "Target and Walmart and Amazon, corporations whose principal interest in Berks County is how to take money out of it." The sermon claims that the local community has resources of its own: the stars above us, the word given to us, the meal. These gifts exist on a scale too small or remote for the kingdom of the world to appreciate: a point of light, a book, a loaf of bread and a single cup. To the people of God, however, they are an abundant harvest. I would also argue that the sermon is rhetorically strongest on the final page when it seeks to draw its auditors into a more profound sense of membership—the idea that each of us reflects Christ's light into the community in a unique way.

Finally, it is not insignificant that this sermon points us towards the table in its final paragraphs. Holy Communion is, of course, an ultimate expression of local community, proper scale, and membership. In the context of this sermon, though, it is more: it is a reminder that our worship of God, though it occurs indoors, always takes place within the context of God's Great Economy. Bread and wine are not fundamentally items we buy in a store: they are the fruit of the field and the vine; they are constituted of earth and water and light. They may be brought indoors, but they are made up of outdoor "stuff," and as such they bind us to God's greater purposes. These manifold meanings are especially evident to people who have the good fortune to receive in their hands each week bread that has been freshly baked by members of the congregation.

This sermon seems to me to reflect faithfully on a large handful of agrarian themes and concerns. It is not the whole picture, but then no sermon is the whole picture. Preachers never say everything they intend precisely as they intend. Congregations do not understand or remember all they are told, and they often understand differently from the intentions of the preacher. What matters is not perfection but fidelity. We abide with each other. We gather in a particular time and place, embrace each other in a shared membership, walk in a common story, worship together, sing together, and eat together. The crucified one is among us—the Good Shepherd, the Lord of the Harvest, the Alpha and the Omega. And to our endless astonishment, to our eternal delight, we find that we ourselves have been made Christ's harvest.

Bibliography

Allen, Ronald J. *Patterns of Preaching: A Sermon Sampler*. St. Louis: Chalice, 1998.

Angyal, Andrew J. *Wendell Berry*. Twayne's United States Author Series, No. 654. New York: Twayne, 1995.

Berry, Wendell. *Andy Catlett: Early Education*. Monterey, KY: Larkspur, 2010.

———. *Andy Catlett: Early Travels*. Washington, DC: Shoemaker & Hoard, 2006.

———. *Another Turn of the Crank*. Washington, DC: Counterpoint, 1995.

———. *The Art of Loading Brush*. Berkeley: Counterpoint, 2017.

———. *The Art of the Commonplace: The Agrarian Essays of Wendell Berry*. Washington, DC: Counterpoint, 2002.

———. *Bringing It to the Table*. Berkeley: Counterpoint, 2009.

———. *Citizenship Papers*. Washington, DC: Shoemaker & Hoard, 2003.

———. *Collected Poems: 1957–1982*. San Francisco: North Point, 1984.

———. *The Country of Marriage*. New York: Harcourt Brace Jovanovich, 1973.

———. *The Discovery of Kentucky*. Frankfort, KY: Gnomon, 1991.

———. *Farming: A Handbook*. San Diego: Harcourt Brace Jovanovich, 1970.

———. *Fidelity*. New York: Pantheon, 1992.

———. *The Gift of Good Land: Further Essays Cultural and Agricultural*. New York: North Point, 1981.

———. *Given: Poems*. Washington, DC: Shoemaker & Hoard, 2005.

———. *Hannah Coulter*. Washington, DC: Shoemaker & Hoard, 2004.

———. *Harlan Hubbard: The Blazer Lectures for 1989*. Lexington, KY: University Press of Kentucky, 1990.

———. *Home Economics: Fourteen Essays*. San Francisco: North Point, 1987.

———. *Imagination in Place*. Berkeley: Counterpoint, 2010.

———. *In the Presence of Fear: Three Essays for a Changed World*. Great Barrington, MA: The Orion Society, 2001.

———. *It All Turns on Affection: The Jefferson Lecture and Other Essays*. Berkeley: Counterpoint, 2012.

———. *Jayber Crow: The Life Story of Jayber Crow, Barber, of the Port William Membership, as Written by Himself: A Novel*. Washington, DC: Counterpoint, 2000.

———. *Leavings: Poems*. Berkeley: Counterpoint, 2010.

———. *Life Is a Miracle: An Essay against Modern Superstition*. Washington, DC: Counterpoint, 2000.

———. *The Mad Farmer Poems*. Berkeley: Counterpoint, 2014.

———. *The Memory of Old Jack*. San Diego: Harcourt, Brace & Company, 1974.

———. *Nathan Coulter—Revised Edition*. San Francisco: North Point, 1985.

———. *New Collected Poems*. Berkeley: Counterpoint, 2012.

———. *Openings*. New York: Harcourt Brace Jovanovich, 1968.

———. *Our Only World: Ten Essays*. Berkeley: Counterpoint, 2015.

———. *A Part*. San Francisco: North Point, 1980.

———. *A Place in Time: Twenty Stories of the Port William Membership*. Berkeley: Counterpoint, 2012.

———. *A Place on Earth (Revision)*. New York: North Point, 1983.

———. *Recollected Essays: 1965–1980*. New York: North Point, 1981.

———. *Remembering*. San Francisco: North Point, 1988.

———. *Roots to the Earth*. Berkeley: Counterpoint, 2014.

———. *Sabbaths 2006*. Monterey, KY: Larkspur, 2008.

———. *Sayings and Doings and An Eastward Look*. Frankfort, KY: Gnomon, n.d.

———. *The Selected Poems of Wendell Berry*. Berkeley: Counterpoint, 1998.

———. *Sex, Economy, Freedom and Community: Eight Essays*. New York: Pantheon, 1993.

———. *A Small Porch: Sabbath Poems 2014 and 2015 Together with The Presence of Nature in the Natural World: A Long Conversation*. Berkeley: Counterpoint, 2016.

———. *Standing on Earth: Selected Essays*. Ipswich: Golgonooza, 1991.

———. *Standing by Words*. New York: North Point, 1983.

———. *That Distant Land: The Collected Stories*. Washington, DC: Shoemaker & Hoard, 2004.

———. *This Day: Sabbath Poems, Collected and New, 1979–2013*. Berkeley: Counterpoint, 2013.

———. *A Timbered Choir: The Sabbath Poems 1979–2007*. Washington, DC: Counterpoint, 1998.

———. *Traveling at Home*. Berkeley: Counterpoint, 1998.

———. *Two More Stories of the Port William Membership*. Gnomon Chapbooks Series 4. Frankfort, KY: Gnomon, 1994.

———. *The Unsettling of America: Culture and Agriculture*. San Francisco: Sierra Club, 1977.

———. *Watch with Me and Six Other Stories of the Yet-Remembered Ptolemy Proudfoot and His Wife Miss Minnie, Nee Quinch*. New York: Pantheon, 1994.

———. *The Way of Ignorance and Other Essays*. Washington, DC: Shoemaker & Hoard, 2005.

———. *What Are People For?* New York: North Point, 1990.

———. *What Matters?: Economics for a Renewed Commonwealth*. Berkeley: Counterpoint, 2010.

———. *Whitefoot: A Story from the Center of the World*. Berkeley: Counterpoint, 2009.

———. *The Wild Birds: Six Stories of the Port William Membership*. San Francisco: North Point, 1985.

———. *Window Poems*. Emeryville, CA: Shoemaker & Hoard, 2007.

———. *A World Lost*. Washington, DC: Counterpoint, 1996.

———. *The World-Ending Fire: The Essential Wendell Berry*. Westminster: Allen Lane, 2017.

Berry, Wendell, et al. *Citizens Dissent: Security, Morality, and Leadership in an Age of Terror: Essays*. Great Barrington, MA: Orion Society, 2003.

Berry, Wendell, and Morris Allen Grubbs. *Conversations with Wendell Berry*. Literary Conversations Series. Jackson, MI: University Press of Mississippi, 2007.

Blessed Are the Peacemakers: Christ's Teachings about Love, Compassion and Forgiveness Gathered and Introduced by Wendell Berry. Washington, DC: Shoemaker & Hoard, 2005.

Bonzo, J. Matthew, and Michael R. Stevens. *Wendell Berry and the Cultivation of Life: A Reader's Guide*. Grand Rapids: Brazos, 2008.

Davis, Ellen F. *Scripture, Culture, and Agriculture: An Agrarian Reading of the Bible*. New York: Cambridge University Press, 2009.

Donahue, John R. *The Gospel in Parable: Metaphor, Narrative, and Theology in the Synoptic Gospels*. Philadelphia: Fortress, 1988.

Dulles, Avery. *Models of the Church*. New York: Doubleday, 1987.

"Earth Day Journal: Volume One." Earth Day Journal. New Castle, KY: The Berry Center, 2018.

Forde, Gerhard O. *On Being a Theologian of the Cross: Reflections on Luther's Heidelberg Disputation, 1518*. Grand Rapids: Eerdmans, 1997.

Freedman, Russell. *Wendell Berry: A Bibliography*. Occasional Papers, No. 12. Lexington, KY: University of Kentucky Libraries, 1998.

Grubbs, Morris Allen, ed. *Conversations with Wendell Berry*. Literary Conversation Series. Jackson, MS: University Press of Mississippi, 2007.

Hall, Douglas John. *The End of Christendom and the Future of Christianity*. Valley Forge, PA: Trinity, 1997.

———. *God and Human Suffering: An Exercise in the Theology of the Cross*. Minneapolis: Augsburg, 1986.

———. *Hope against Hope: Towards an Indigenous Theology of the Cross*. Vol. 1, no. 3. Tokyo: WSCF, 1971.

Jackson, Wes. *New Roots for Agriculture*. New ed. Lincoln: University of Nebraska Press, 1985.

Jackson, Wes, et al. *Meeting the Expectations of the Land: Essays in Sustainable Agriculture and Stewardship*. San Francisco: North Point, 1984.

Lathrop, Gordon W. *Holy Things: A Liturgical Theology*. Minneapolis: Fortress, 1993.

Lewis, C. S. *The Discarded Image*. New York: Cambridge University Press, 1964.

Lewis, Karoline. *John*. Fortress Biblical Preaching Commentaries. Minneapolis: Fortress, 2014.

Lischer, Richard. *Reading the Parables*. Interpretation: Resources for the Use of Scripture in the Church. Louisville, KY: Westminster John Knox, 2014.

Lowry, Eugene L. *The Homiletical Plot, Expanded Edition: The Sermon as Narrative Art Form*. Louisville, KY: John Knox, 2001.

Luther, Martin. *The Annotated Luther, Volume 1: The Roots of Reformation*. Timothy J. Wengert, ed. Minneapolis: Fortress, 2015.

Merchant, Paul, ed. *Wendell Berry*. Confluence American Authors Series. Lewiston, ID: Confluence, 1991.

Moltmann, Jürgen. *The Crucified God*. 40th anniv. ed. Minneapolis: Fortress, 2015.

Paulson, Steven D. *Lutheran Theology*. New York: T. & T. Clark, 2011.

Peters, Jason, ed. *Wendell Berry: Life and Work*. Culture of the Land. Lexington, KY: University Press of Kentucky, 2007.

Prenter, Regin. *Luther's Theology of the Cross*. Historical Series 17 (Reformation). Philadelphia: Fortress, 1971.

Scott, Bernard Brandon. *Hear Then the Parable: A Commentary on the Parables of Jesus*. Minneapolis: Fortress, 1989.

Shuman, Joel James, and L. Roger Owen, eds. *Wendell Berry and Religion: Heaven's Earthly Life*. Lexington, KY: University Press of Kentucky, 2009.

Smith, Kimberly K. *Wendell Berry and the Agrarian Tradition: A Common Grace*. Lawrence, KS: University Press of Kansas, 2003.

"Special Issue: Wendell Berry." *Christianity and Literature* 56 2 (2007).

Sutterfield, Ragan. *Wendell Berry and the Given Life*. Cincinnati: Franciscan Media, 2017.

Thompson, Virgil. *Justification Is for Preaching: Essays by Oswald Bayer, Gerhard O. Forde, and Others*. Eugene, OR: Pickwick, 2012.

Tisdale, Leonora Tubbs. *Preaching as Local Theology and Folk Art*. Minneapolis: Fortress, 1997.

Wiebe, Joseph R. *The Place of Imagination: Wendell Berry and the Poetics of Community, Affection, and Identity*. Waco, TX: Baylor University Press, 2017.

Wirzba, Norman, ed. *The Art of the Commonplace: The Agrarian Essays of Wendell Berry*. Washington, DC: Counterpoint, 2002.

www.ingramcontent.com/pod-product-compliance
Lightning Source LLC
Chambersburg PA
CBHW020210090426
42734CB00008B/1003